GANDHI

GANDHI

by Olivia Coolidge

Houghton Mifflin Company Boston 1971

Books by

OLIVIA COOLIDGE

Caesar's Gallic War
Come By Here
Cromwell's Head
Egyptian Adventures
George Bernard Shaw
Greek Myths
The King of Men
Legends of the North
Lives of Famous Romans
The Maid of Artemis
Makers of the Red Revolution
Marathon Looks on the Sea
Men of Athens
People in Palestine
Roman People
Tales of the Crusades
The Trojan War
Winston Churchill and the Story
of Two World Wars

CONTENTS

GANDHI

Introduction

To the people of India he was the Mahatma, the "Great Soul." To the Indian Republic he is Father of the Nation. To his disciples he was Bapu, simply "Father." To the Western world he is the saint of nonviolence, the man who led a revolution without war. Yet this "Great Soul" was capable of rages, of arrogance, of error. The Father of the Nation made mistakes in judgment to which the partition of India is partly due. Bapu could fail in tenderness toward his own sons. The saint of nonviolence was a fighting man; and his revolution encouraged violence elsewhere.

Gandhi like all saints was a human being; but he lived in an age when it was possible to record more things about him than ever have been known of another saint. During a fast, for instance, All-India Radio told millions how many ounces of water he drank and how many ounces of urine he passed, the state of his pulse, or when he was given an enema. These details were matched by incredible collections of his writings: newspaper articles, pamphlets, posters, personal letters in such an unending stream that, despite his use of dictation, he had taught himself to write with the left hand when the other grew tired. Countless photographs add to a collection that is swollen to still vaster proportions by reminiscences from what appears to be everyone who ever knew him.

From such a mass of detail a man emerges who is more interesting than a saint or a great soul or even the father of a country. We can see that Gandhi really was all these things and that if he had lived in an era when records were less comprehensive, it would have been easier to compare him with other saints or patriots or even revolutionaries, simply because we should have met him on those terms.

As things are, anyone who studies the life of Gandhi must be struck by the human size of his weaknesses. He had superb gifts and energies, but he also had nervous states and failures of temper or judgment. These parts of the whole man are so intermingled that if one were to remove the blemishes, one would destroy the saint. Like the toothless smile or the cheap watch, they are parts of the picture, without which the whole makes no sense. It begins to dawn on us that other saintly men must have been like this, had we but known them better. Saintliness and greatness are expressed through personality, but they do not flatten out the bumps or smooth the distortions. On occasion they even exaggerate these by making foibles unduly important which in a lesser man would not be noticed.

We can even go so far as to see in the case of Gandhi that qualities that we might describe as human failings have a positive side and help to convey his whole message. Intellectually, for instance, Gandhi was limited to seeing what he wanted to see. As a result, the economic future that he planned for India was an impractical one. His contempt for modern medicine or the basic scientific rules of nutrition made a good deal of his personal advice to others absurd. Yet these eccentricities present a genuine challenge to the assumptions of Western civilization. Gandhi's valid criticisms are made more vivid by his lofty, almost ludicrous contempt for certain facts. A great part of his message to the Western world is that modern science is not the ultimate judge of human values, that the Christian religion is not the only way of approaching God, and that in general the assumptions on which we base our lives need much rethinking.

Part of the greatness of Gandhi is an extraordinary concentration, combined with the power to be unusually diverse. In one sense he is always the same: the little man with the rigid schedule spins so much every day, goes through a regular routine of brisk walk, meditation, bath, massage and weekly day of silence. He even imposes a similar regimen on anybody who is rash enough to want to live with him. Into this framework, however, Gandhi fitted the activities of patriot, revolutionary, religious and social reformer, doctor, economist, statesman, politician, adding to all of them an intense interest in his own and other people's spiritual welfare. It is thus impossible to sum him up or reach the end of him, for his weakness in the economic sphere may be a part of his spiritual strength, and a failure in political negotiation may mark his success as a Hindu reformer.

One thing we can say of him. Though intensely human, he was not like other men, because he was never ordinary. Just as his appearance, though odd, was unmistakable, so his personality was unique, not in the imperceptible way that our fingerprints are unique, but openly, obviously so. We shall not look upon his like again. Humanity is richer for having produced him, richer in spiritual values and in wide diversity, richer through the demonstration of how great man can be and how much he can accomplish. This surely is what Nehru meant when he spoke to Gandhi's own people, saying, "A thousand years later that light will still be seen in this country, and the world will see it, and it will give solace to innumerable hearts."

Little Mohan

MOHANDAS KARAMCHAND GANDHI was born on the second
of October, 1869, at Porbandar, a pretty, white-walled sea-
port on the coast of Kathiawar, the huge blunt peninsula
that is conspicuous on the western coast of India. Had he
been any ordinary child, this one event would have settled
his future, since birth in Hindu India determines caste, while
caste in its turn prescribes whom one may marry, with whom
one may share a meal, whom one may touch, and to a large
extent what trade one may pursue. There are some three
thousand castes in India, all subdivisions of four original
groups: the Brahmans, or scholars; the warriors or rulers; the
traders; and the peasants. The Gandhi family belonged to
a division of the trading class, as can be easily understood
from its surname Gandhi, which is a common one in India
and means "grocer."

Karamchand Gandhi, the father of little Mohandas, was
not as it happened a grocer. For the previous couple of centuries the family had been in government service in Kathi-

awar, and Karamchand was at this time chief minister in the principality of Porbandar. This sounds important, but in fact the state consisted of a single town with a little country around it and contained some 72,000 inhabitants in all. The administration of British India was peculiar. The important parts were British provinces, but there were also over six hundred native princes who did as they pleased with their own subjects, checked only by British advisers in cases of outrageous misgovernment. Porbandar possessed a white stone palace and a prince and a court, as well as a chief minister. Karamchand Gandhi lived in a three-story white stone building that looked imposing and had been strong enough to stand a siege in an earlier generation when the then regent had quarreled with Karamchand's father.

Like everything else about Porbandar, Karamchand's dwelling was not as magnificent as it appeared. He shared it with his five brothers and their families, so that his own family quarters consisted of two rooms with a tiny kitchen and verandah. Neither Karamchand nor his father had squeezed out a fortune for himself; all went to the Prince. Moreover, as successor to his father's position, Karamchand was expected to provide for his brothers. He did so by giving them jobs in the Prince's service; but his private fortune, such as it was, would also be at their disposal if money were needed, as for instance to marry their sons. All this meant modest living but a warm relationship and plenty of cousins for little Mohan to play with.

Karamchand Gandhi had not had luck with his first three wives. They had been ailing and had not borne him sons. He was forty when he married Putliba, who was about thirteen, a conventional age for a Hindu girl to marry. Mohan was her fourth child and third son, born nine or ten years later when his father was nearly fifty, in Indian terms an old man. The little boy was younger than his cousins and seems to have been a family pet. He always had great charm; and he liked his own way, which he usually got, though sometimes this meant mischief. All the same, it was made clear to him from babyhood that life was serious to grown-up people. His elderly father, very much the head of his family, was a sober, upright man with no taste for display. It is recorded of him that he used to sit in his courtyard resolving disputes between the Prince's subjects while peeling the vegetables for his wife's kitchen. Though uneducated by any modern standard, he had a deep interest in religious thought. The Prince's family was Muslim, descending from the Mogul conquerors who had ruled India before the British came. Karamchand was drawn into discussions of Muslim beliefs, and he also encouraged relationships with Jain monks, Hindu pacifists who believed in hurting no living thing, not even an insect. The Gandhi family, as is common though not universal among Hindus, was vegetarian.

Mohan was devoted to his young mother. Putliba Gandhi was a strong personality with a quiet, loving disposition. In India, the family capital often consisted of its women's jewelry. Putliba wore heavy silver anklets like every other woman of her class. She even had gold-washed bracelets and wore a gold nose ring on special occasions. But these were simple adornments for the chief minister's wife, the more especially as she was highly respected by the ladies of the court. Her dress was plain at all times. She was deeply religious in a far more personal way than her husband. Next door was a temple of the god Krishna, worshiped as an incarnation of Vishnu, the Protector, one of the three great gods of the Hindu Trinity. Idol worship is widely practiced in India as a suitable way of approaching the Divine Being for simple, uneducated souls. Gandhi himself never cared for it, but the ritual suited Putliba's temperament. She went to the temple almost daily, often taking her small son, who was rather frightened by the dark place and the staring images or the chanting of the priests as they went through the ritual of Krishna's day. Putliba also practiced many austerities to gain spiritual strength, fasting regularly in the rainy season as well as on other occasions. Mohan always remembered how she took a vow one rainy season that she would not eat until she saw the sun. The sun does not often appear during monsoon rains, so the children would watch for a break in the clouds and rush in to tell her. Putliba would come out to see for herself; but by then the clouds had sometimes closed again. "God does not intend me to eat today," she would say, calmly going back to her duties.

To such parents, the world was a serious place; yet family life was not unhappy. Actually it has always been difficult to gain a rounded picture of Mohan's childhood. Most of what we know rests on reminiscences that he himself wrote down after he was fifty; and the incidents that he selects are intended to show how he thought his character had developed. At least, however, Gandhi is reliable. Other people who had known the great man in childhood tried later to see in him the person that he grew up to be, with the result that stories were given a twist which may remind us of Washington and the cherry tree. The little boy was pictured as being unnaturally fearless, truthful, and good from the very beginning.

Of course this was not so. Mohan seems to have been lively, with a strong sense of mischief, a will of his own, and a sensitive disposition that was easily frightened by disapproval. He was an odd-looking child with big sticking-out ears, thick nose, and heavy mouth. His neck was as thin as a stalk, and his mop of black hair was unruly. But his plainness was redeemed by a delightful smile and a pair of fine eyes that often twinkled. Physically he was small and frail-looking; and he describes himself as very timid, frightened of the dark until well into his teens, terrified of snakes, avoiding rough sports, and weeping easily. Yet when he was old enough to perceive these faults in himself, he did not accept them. We soon become conscious of a driving energy in him and an ambition to be great, heroic, and masterful. In all of these things he succeeded.

When Mohan was seven years old, his father left Porbandar after a dispute with its ruler and was appointed chief minister to Rajkot state, a hundred and twenty miles inland, leaving his own ancestral post to his brother Tulsidas. Rajkot, though smaller than Porbandar and less attractive, was important because it served the British as an administrative center for the whole district. For a couple of years Karamchand lived there alone, leaving his wife and children in Porbandar. When he moved them, Mohan was sent to

The main entrance
of the house at Rajkot
where Gandhi spent
part of his childhood

primary school in Rajkot. He had apparently already learned his letters in Gujarati, which was the language spoken all over the Kathiawar peninsula. The Rajkot primary school, however, was more elaborate than the one available in Porbandar. By modern standards, it was not much. The subjects were arithmetic, Gujarati, and the geography of India. Not all the teachers were qualified; all facts were learned by rote; writing was done on slates. Still, school was not bad, although Mohan never made many friends among his classmates, preferring to run home at the end of the day to play by himself. Perhaps the Rajkot children looked on him as a foreigner. In any case, his primary schooling only lasted for two years. The Kathiawar High School, to which he then moved, was a bigger and more modern place, endowed by local rulers to serve the district as a whole. The school's very size was hard on a shy boy, but the worst thing about it was that instruction was given in English.

In later life, Gandhi always blamed the British for imposing on India a foreign education in a totally strange language. The criticism is sound, but there was something to be said for the British point of view. There are more languages in India than in Europe, and none of them have either the vocabulary or the concepts needed to convey Western thought. As he grew older, Gandhi grew increasingly critical of academic education, but even he drew up a scheme for India in which he prescribed five languages in high school, airily explaining that after the first two, the rest would be easy and that steady application for a short time every day would solve all problems. Later on, the committee that drew up the Indian constitution after independence was unable to express its ideas in Hindustani without hopelessly mangling a language that had not developed idioms for such a task.

The trouble was that in actual practice high-school instruction in English, especially when delivered by Indian teachers who did not themselves know the language well, was a disaster. Young Mohan loathed high school, where he spent seven years; and he later complained that he had no aptitude and might have done better without formal education. This was, however, a gross exaggeration. It is true that his record was erratic, but this was not even mainly owing to instruction in English. High school simply came at a time when the boy had important things to settle within himself.

He seems to have been about twelve when he first began to question the rigid rules that directed Hindu life. The family employed a scavenger called Uka to clean out their latrines. This was a duty that no caste Hindu could perform without pollution. It was always entrusted to an outcaste with whom even the family servants would not associate. Uka's touch was a pollution, and even the vessels that he had handled could never be used by other men. Mohan began to ask why he had to cleanse himself and say special prayers if he accidentally brushed against Uka. Was not the scavenger a man like everybody else? Mohan actually liked him. Putliba had no good answer for her son, though surely the question was raised as a result of her own life and example. To her, custom was part of religion and taken for granted. Resourcefully she pointed out that if Mohan did not like the purification rites, he could pass on his pollution to a non-Hindu by touching him. There were plenty of Muslims in high school who were outside the caste system, so that the child was silenced for the moment.

Presently he started to smoke secretly with a cousin. This was not strictly speaking a sin to Hindus, but it was certainly frowned upon by the sect devoted to Vishnu, to which the Gandhis belonged. For a while the boys were able to manage by collecting butts scattered by an uncle. When butts ran out, they tried other leaves with small success. Eventually Mohan stole money to buy cigarettes. This soon put both boys in an unbearable position. When the cigarettes were gone, they dared not steal again. Neither had the courage to confess, but their deceit was so awful that they could not live with it. They decided on suicide. In a businesslike way they collected some seeds from the datura plant, which is highly narcotic. They went to the temple and performed the rites proper to people who are about to end their lives. Then they retired to a quiet place and gingerly ate a few of the seeds. Nothing seemed to happen. They wondered if datura really was a poison and how many seeds they ought to eat. It occurred to both of them that they did not much want to die. Perhaps if they made offerings in the temple, they could put themselves right with the gods and start again. This seemed a good plan, and with relief it was adopted.

The actual scrape was not remarkable. Countless other little boys have done similar things, but few of them have been driven seriously to think of suicide. Nothing shows more clearly the puritan standards of the household and the suffering that a sensitive boy might have to go through in the process of making up his own mind. Adolescence for Mohan would have been difficult in any case. At this point, however, his father complicated matters by deciding that he was to get married at the age of thirteen.

For an Indian boy this was certainly young, but sixteen was normal. Mohan's brother Karsandas was about that age, and there was a cousin who was ready also. Indian marriages are the occasion for an enormous family feast that is ruinously expensive, so much so that weddings are considered one of the chief reasons why the peasantry and the artisan class sink into debt. It seemed common sense to the Gandhis to marry the three boys off at one time in order to save money on the wedding party.

Mohan had already been betrothed for six years to the daughter of a merchant of the same caste who lived a few doors away in Porbandar. Parents made these arrangements early on, and actually Mohan had been betrothed before, at least once, possibly twice. Child mortality ran high, especially among girls, who generally received less care than their brothers. Presumably at seven Mohan was told that he was going to marry Kasturbai Makanji at some distant date, just as earlier he had been going to marry another little girl. It was not important news to him and apparently did not even arouse a desire to take a look at Kasturbai, though he knew her family well and may have seen her. She was within a few days of his own age, had had no schooling, but had been brought up in more luxurious surroundings than the Gandhis.

He had plenty of time to get excited now because wedding preparations consumed months. Jewels and fine clothes were bought. Families exchanged costly presents. Big feasts were planned. Horses, cooks, and servants had to be hired. The weddings were to be held at Porbandar because all the connections of both families were there. Any other arrangement would have been unthinkable.

Unfortunately the ruler of Rajkot had such a high value for Karamchand's services that he did not want to let him go for the occasion. He could hardly refuse outright; but the celebrations were going to take a week, and leisurely travel to Porbandar by bullock cart would consume five days. The family was sent ahead to preside over preparations, while the ruler provided a stagecoach for Karamchand, giving instructions that it should leave at the last minute and get over the ground as quickly as possible. These orders were obeyed, but the road was too rough for fast travel. Not far from Porbandar, the coach overturned; and the minister, now in his sixties, was thrown out. He did manage to preside over the weddings swathed in bandages, but some of the joy went out of the occasion.

Mohan was not greatly concerned with his father's injuries. He regarded Karamchand with respect and awe, but at the moment he was fully occupied with what was going on. It was fun to be dressed up like a little prince, to be the center of attention, to have to ride a horse to fetch Kasturbai, to be coached in all the ceremonial details of the wedding. Besides, it was now explained that a bride was not merely a playmate for him to order about as he pleased. The idea of sex was exciting, but troubling at thirteen. No wonder he was nervous, eager, absorbed in his role. In later life he remembered the occasion as one on which he thought of little but himself.

Everything went off as it should. The undersized boy and his even tinier bride sat together on a platform, dressed up like a pair of dolls. The priests sang hymns, and a great feast was set for the relations. Presently the pair arose and made seven steps together, symbolizing their progress through all stages of life. They offered one another sweet cakes to symbolize joy. They joined in the feasting and were escorted to their marriage chamber.

The effect of marriage on Mohan's schoolwork was disastrous because it gave him so many emotional problems. It was not that he did not like Kasturbai; on the contrary, he liked her too well. She was a tiny person, daintily made and only reaching to the shoulder of her husband, who never grew beyond five foot five. Her photographs at a later age suggest that she may have been pretty in a charming, delicate way that faded early. Her upbringing had taught her

that a Hindu wife's duty was to please her husband in all
things, but she had a will of her own and had been perhaps
indulged at home. Mohan, thrown off balance, was emo-
tionally demanding and wildly jealous at the same time. He
wanted her all to himself and forbade her to go out of doors,
even to the temple, without his permission. He was after all
no older than she, and no wiser. They quarreled and made
love and quarreled again, while Mohan found out painfully
that a wife is not a plaything or a slave, but another person.

He could not, for instance, teach her to read. She did not
see the use of it; and he went at the matter too hard, demanding too much. She did not attend. There was no end to the
problems of marriage.

Sex was the greatest of these. They had both been introduced to it too early, and it swept Mohan away. In later life
he spoke of his thirteen-year-old marriage as a great injury
that his father had unintentionally done him. He attributed
to it a wasted year; and it gave him a feeling, which persisted
all his life, that sex consumed energy that ought to be
devoted to more positive things. He was obsessed with Kasturbai and grew resentful of being so because he was certain
that there were more important things in life.

Actually, though the pattern of his adolescence had been
violently disturbed, it had not been destroyed. He was still
exploring his world, assessing the value of the traditions of
his parents. In the course of doing so, he made a friend,
Sheikh Mehtab, a Muslim, three years older and one of the
best athletes of the Kathiawar High School. It was a queer
attraction of opposites. Mohan admired in Mehtab many
qualities he himself lacked: poise, physical courage, and ath-
letic build. Mehtab in his turn seems to have enjoyed domi-
nating the younger boy and chose to sneer at the restrictions
imposed upon Hindus. Mohan ought to eat meat. English-

men did, and so did Muslims and even some Hindus. He
quoted a piece of doggerel that a Gujarati poet had written:

> *Behold the mighty Englishman,*
> *He rules the Indian small,*
> *Because being a meat-eater*
> *He is five cubits tall.*

Some biographers have pointed out that Gandhi's struggle
with the English really began at this moment. Actually, for
more than half his lifetime he was proud of being a British
subject. It is true, however, that he already did aspire to be
as good as anyone, including the English; and if acquiring
extra cubits through eating meat was the way to achieve this,
he was ready to overcome his nausea.

This did not prove easy. The first meat meal had to be
taken in secret, and Mehtab was not a good cook over a
campfire. Mohan forced down a meal of goat's meat, tough
as leather; and then predictably he threw it up. That night
he was awakened by a nightmare about a live goat bleating
in his stomach. Mehtab, however, persisted, deciding that
restaurants were safe from Mohan's family. Restaurant meals
went better; but since Mehtab had to pay, such extrava-
gances were not frequent. Mohan never got an extra cubit
of stature, but he did decide that it was foolish to be a vegetarian. The deception of his family, however, continued to
bother him. At last he found courage to tell Mehtab he
would wait until he was grown up and his own master, when
he would openly eat meat. He was maturing.

His friendship with Mehtab continued. He was led into
other scrapes, and so was his brother Karsandas, Mehtab's
age. Presently Karsandas found himself in debt. Disaster
threatened unless he could find twenty-five rupees. Between

them, Karsandas and Mehtab persuaded Mohan to carve a piece out of a gold armlet that was worn by Karsandas and sell it. The debt was paid off, but Mohan's conscience would not rest. This time he was brave enough to resolve on confessing to his father. He wrote out a confession and gave it to the old man, who was at this time confined to bed. Karamchand had never recovered from his accident completely, and in addition he was suffering from a fistula.

The boy was prepared to face anger and blows, but Karamchand wept as he read what was written, and then tore the paper up. His forgiveness and the boy's repentance opened a deep understanding between the two for the first time. Respect for a father is one of the first duties of a Hindu, but from this moment Mohan was conscious of being loved, and in return he gave devotion.

There were plenty of ways to express his new feeling because Karamchand was really gravely ill. His fistula grew worse, and doctors of all faiths were called in for consultations. There was even a question of an operation in Bombay, but Karamchand's personal doctor spoke against it. Mohan did a great deal of nursing as his father's strength ebbed away. He massaged his legs to relieve some of the pain, gave him medicines, or simply sat by his bedside watching and waiting to fulfill his slightest need. Most of his leisure hours after school were spent this way, and possibly Karamchand thought that he indeed had a model son. Privately Mohan did not agree. Even while he served his father, his thoughts were with Kasturbai, who was carrying his first child. He was as obsessed with her as ever.

In November of 1885, when he was just sixteen, he sat up late with his father one evening, longing for Kasturbai. At last one of his uncles came in to sit by the bedside, and

Mohan was only too glad to slip away. But he had not been with his wife more than five or six minutes when he was urgently called back, too late. His father had died.

It was a terrible shock. He could not forgive himself for having waited so impatiently to get away. A few weeks later his child was born and died after a few days. He blamed himself for this also. His whole relationship with Kasturbai had been wrong from the beginning. Sensitive, morbid, overburdened by emotions he could not master, conscious of aspirations he did not understand how to fulfill, Mohandas Gandhi at sixteen years of age was far from ready to take on the responsibilities of adult life.

A Vegetarian in London

THE DEATH of Karamchand Gandhi left his family badly off. Despite his simple life, the minister had saved little money, and his lingering illness had consumed a great deal of it. The Prince of Rajkot, who had allowed him a small pension when he grew too ill to work, now saw no reason to go on supporting a family that contained three young men, all capable of earning. There could be no question of Laxmidas, the eldest son, succeeding to his father's position. He was only twenty-two and had not had any opportunity to learn the job.

For a while the family stayed in Rajkot, living partly at least from sums paid by the uncles in rent for the house in Porbandar. Mohandas had nearly two years of high school to finish and made great efforts to do better. At the beginning of his last year he stood fourth in his class and won a small scholarship. His ambition was to become a doctor because he had been impressed by the Bombay surgeon who had advised an operation for his father. Accordingly, when he had graduated from high school, he went on to college. There was a newly founded college some ninety miles off, which he entered in January 1888, leaving Kasturbai behind with the family in Rajkot.

In five months he was home again, a failure. Either his preparation had been inadequate, or else accumulated strains had driven him into a minor breakdown. He had wasted time and much-needed family money, while his wife had added to his burdens by giving birth to their first son, Harilal.

Mohan's eldest brother Laxmidas had the responsibility of deciding what to do about him. According to Indian custom, family property is owned by all the family together, but the head of the family controls its use. Laxmidas had agreed to Mohan's finishing high school and then going on to college. Now the question was whether to invest more money in him or find him a job. Laxmidas suggested consulting an elderly priest called Mavji Dave, who had long been a family friend and was a respected man throughout Kathiawar. The priest thought little of the idea of going to college, pointing out that a degree would qualify Mohan for nothing but a second-rate job in the civil service, from which he would never rise to a top post, since these were reserved for Europeans. What Mohan ought to be preparing for was his father's position as the chief minister in Rajkot. But times had changed; it was no longer possible to inherit such a post, or even to train for it by apprenticeship. One must be qualified. "What Mohan needs to do," urged Mavji Dave, "is go to London and get a law degree. It will take three years and cost five thousand rupees." He added good advice about seeking scholarships from Porbandar and elsewhere, warning, however, that there might be opposition to the plan on religious grounds.

Gandhi (right) with his brother Laxmidas in 1886

Mohan was wildly eager. He had already thought long-
ingly of London and of training in one of its great hospitals.
As a doctor, he could have served humanity; but the prospect
of being such a man as his father was also appealing, especially when combined with this adventure. That Mohan
should have wished to go is hardly surprising; it is more
remarkable that Laxmidas should have agreed.

Unquestionably the priest's advice weighed heavily, but
Laxmidas, as head of the family, was bound to consider the
proposal. It soon became obvious that five thousand rupees
would not be enough. Ten thousand was suggested, and in

the long run the adventure cost thirteen. No scholarships were forthcoming from Porbandar or Rajkot. Uncles and cousins who might have helped objected that Mohan would be breaking the rules of his caste by going overseas. In these circumstances, there was no way to find the money except to sell the family property and Kasturbai's jewels. In other words, Laxmidas was asked to invest all the family resources in a single member; and it was up to him to decide whether Mohandas would be profitable from the family's point of view.

When Gandhi in later life talks of himself as a poor student with little aptitude, we need to remember Laxmidas. Somehow or other Mohan had impressed himself on his brother, perhaps by the tireless energy for which he never gives himself full credit. Laxmidas did not see himself as going to England, as stepping into his father's shoes, as becoming the financial mainstay of the family and its distinguished man. He was qualified to act as a lawyer's clerk, and there might be jobs through his uncles. But Mohan was to have the most expensive education that money could buy.

Nobody else approved. Kasturbai wept, not so much for the loss of her jewels, as for the separation from her husband. What would happen to her if he took up with a foreign woman? Her father shared her fears and had to be persuaded. Putliba was even more upset. She made a few inquiries about the life her son would lead, and found to her dismay that meat and alcohol were considered necessities in England. Only too often young Indians had returned with habits that shocked their relations. In her trouble she consulted a Jain monk, long a spiritual adviser to the whole family, who suggested that Mohan swear an oath in his presence to abstain from wine, and women, and meat while he was abroad. By this time, Mohan's enthusiasm for meat seems to have worn off; and in any event he was willing to go to great lengths to satisfy his mother. Putliba's conscience was eased by the solemn vow, but the elders of the caste were still not satisfied. There were also rumbles of disapproval from the uncles, but Mohandas had made up his inflexible mind and was not to be diverted. Early in August 1888, he set out for Bombay, arriving a few days before sailing, accompanied by his brother-in-law, who was to see him off.

Straightaway he was summoned before a court of elders belonging to his caste and presided over by a distant relative and friend of his father. Ocean voyages were forbidden by religion, and a pagan life in London must violate caste rules. In vain Mohan protested that he had taken an oath and would abide by it. The court demanded that he give up his journey. With great courage he refused, though excommunication from the caste would mean separation from all his friends and kin. He was promptly expelled, and members were forbidden to see him off or help him in any way. It was a frightening situation. Even his brother-in-law was afraid to give him the money that had been set aside for his journey. Mohandas was forced to find a friend from another caste and borrow the money, which his brother-in-law paid back, so that in this fashion he could swear he had not given Mohan anything.

Unescorted, therefore, unaided, outcast, but invincibly obstinate, Mohandas Gandhi boarded the S.S. *Clyde* as passenger to London on the twenty-first of August, 1888. He was not yet nineteen years old.

In Bombay he had bought European suits, shirts with stiff collars, and socks and uncomfortable leather shoes instead of sandals. It was probably now that he took his turban off and parted his hair on one side in the European manner. He still looked skinny and small, with features too large for his face. He was terrified, partly out of shyness, but even more so lest ignorance cause him to break his vow. He did not dare to go into the ship's dining room, but tried to live on odds and ends that he had brought with him. Luckily an elderly Indian lawyer who was used to travel had taken the boy into his cabin and kept a kindly eye on him. He understood the problem and persuaded one of the stewards to cook Indian meals. Mohan, who was not used to being on familiar terms with a man so much his elder, could not confide in his companion. He counted his pennies, horrified at how they slipped away from him; and he watched with bright-eyed fascination all the strange things around.

Cautiously he ventured ashore when the ship docked at Aden, Port Said, and Brindisi, but his fears of the unknown were confirmed when he was accosted by a man who wanted to introduce him to "a beautiful girl of fourteen . . . the charge is not high." Carefully he wrote down what to do in his journal — in case he should forget if it happened again.

> "Be calm and answer boldly . . . tell the man to go away . . . If you are in any difficulty, at once refer to a policeman just near you, or at once enter a large building which you will surely see. But before you enter it, read the name on the building and make sure it is open to all . . . Tell the porter that you are in a difficulty, and he will at once show you what you should do . . . By a large building I meant that it must be belonging to Thos. Cook or Henry King or some other such agents . . . Don't be miserly at this time. Pay the porter something."

In other words, be calm and appeal to authority. Mohan's lack of confidence and his agitation prevented him from seeing that he had proved capable of dealing with this fearsome emergency and did not need to make plans for doing so the next time.

By the time that the S.S. *Clyde* had gone through the Suez Canal and reached the Mediterranean, Mohan had overcome his shyness and his difficulties with English sufficiently to make a friend or two among the passengers. To his horror, they all warned him that a vegetarian diet was all very well in tropical India, but would not do in cold weather, which was actually fatal to people who did not build up their resistance with meat and alcohol.

Resignedly he made up his mind to die, but somewhat to his surprise he was as much alive as ever when the ship sailed up the English Channel to anchor at Tilbury in the fog of a raw October day. He had chosen a white tropical suit in which to make his landing, presumably because it was his best. In consequence he must have looked as out of place as he felt. The kindly lawyer took him up to town and established him in a hotel whose gloomy Victorian magnificence was both oppressive and expensive. It being Sunday, Mohan's luggage did not arrive; and the tropical suit marked him as peculiar.

Luckily for his finances, Mohan had an introduction to a distinguished old family friend, who was very helpful. Presently he found himself sharing lodgings with another Indian law student, and then transferring to the home of an Anglo-Indian widow with two daughters. This was a period when English cooking was at its notorious worst. Meals were heavy with roast meats followed by suet puddings made with animal fat. Eggs, fish, and mutton chops appeared at breakfast. Mohandas's first landlady wondered how long he could survive on oatmeal for breakfast, followed by bread, jam and overboiled spinach for dinner or lunch. Nevertheless, it did not occur to her to provide anything better, or even to add the watery milk then common in London. The widow, being an Anglo-Indian, was more sympathetic, though hardly more resourceful. She had at least heard of vegetarian restaurants, but did not know where they were. It began to seem possible that the shipmates on the S.S. *Clyde* had been right. Poor young Mohandas was doomed to die of starvation or tuberculosis, contracted in the damp and cold of his first English winter.

His studies at least were not hard; he had three years to accomplish what took an Englishman with a college degree only a few months with the aid of crammers. Nor did he lack for acquaintances. There was another boy from Rajkot in London studying law, and introductions from one young Indian student to another followed as a matter of course. Mohandas had plenty of people to whom to turn for advice, and they assured him that his most urgent task was to improve his knowledge of English. The best way to do so was to form a regular habit of reading newspapers. Systematically he obeyed and soon became fascinated by the strange new world the papers opened up to him. Meanwhile the simple process of registering as a student in the Inner Temple went through without a hitch.

Everything was being made easy; but he was miserable, bitterly homesick, and obsessed by food. Even his Indian friends told him that a vow made to an illiterate mother with no idea of London conditions ought not to be binding; but it was his link with home, and he could not agree. He brooded endlessly over diet. It was vital to discover the least expensive and most nutritious things to eat. He did not have and never was to acquire any knowledge of the basic principles of nutrition, but the problem assumed an importance in his mind that it never lost.

Walking through the center of London one day, he happened to notice one of the vegetarian restaurants whose whereabouts he had been trying to discover. It was a glorious moment. He went in to have his first full meal since reaching England. What was more, he bought a little pamphlet called *A Plea for Vegetarianism* and made the discovery that an English group claimed eating vegetables was in harmony with Divine Law and man's true nature. He accepted this point of view with joy and never wavered from it. He joined the London Vegetarian Society and began to associate with English people.

It is interesting to see the kind of contact that Gandhi made with Western civilization during these formative years. Owing largely to the personality of their founder, H. S. Salt, the London vegetarians were closely connected with a lively radical movement. Bernard Shaw, by now a dedicated socialist, was a vegetarian and a personal friend of Salt's. The Fabian Society, which was to establish the English welfare state in Gandhi's own lifetime, always contained vegetarians in its ranks, as did the later-formed Labour Party. Pacifism and vegetarianism also went together. It might have been possible for the young man to develop relationships not only with some of the most interesting men of the time, but precisely with those people who were most critical of colonialism. But his interests were not political as yet, and he was not disposed to criticize authority. He would have been tongue-tied by the brilliance of Shaw, yet for all his shyness he was not easily swept away. Thus he only blossomed in the mild ranks of the vegetarians, who soon discovered that despite his diffidence and unimpressive looks, he possessed initiative. As his English improved, he wrote articles for them; he addressed public meetings and founded a vegetarian club near his lodgings.

This was a curious apprenticeship for a future politician, but then Gandhi was in no respect an ordinary man. We may contrast his experience with that of Mohammed Ali Jinnah, the founder of Pakistan and Gandhi's future opponent. Jinnah came to London to study law in 1892 and obtained an introduction, as Gandhi might have done had he wished, to Dadabhai Naoroji, a distinguished Indian living in London who was actually elected to Parliament. Naoroji, who felt an enduring interest in the young potential leaders of his country, took Jinnah under his wing, encouraging him to frequent Parliament and listen to debates. In fact, he gave him a thorough political grounding in British affairs.

Young Gandhi, who only left England about a year before Jinnah arrived, spent his time learning less about politics than about religion. The vegetarians, appealing to Shelley, Thoreau and Ruskin, presented Mohan with a justification of his oath to his mother on general religious grounds. Though highly intelligent, Gandhi was always primarily a practical man who formed opinions because they were useful to him. Vegetarians, moreover, were closely related to freethinking religious groups such as the Theosophists, who drew freely for their doctrines from the religions of the East. Thus precisely the circles in which young Gandhi moved were in a position to discuss, admittedly from strange points of view, the ideas of Hinduism.

Odd though it may appear, at this stage Gandhi knew very little about his own religious background. Hinduism is rigidly demanding in daily life and custom, yet extremely permissive about religious doctrine. A general background belief that is taken for granted considers the human soul as being destined to merge eventually with the Divine. But since it is obvious that almost all human beings are imperfect, sometimes even wicked, and that they are subject to the many temptations of the world, one life is never sufficient to release the soul from bondage to the flesh. Everyone is born again many times to work out his salvation; and on each occasion his position in

life, his caste, his good or bad fortune are a result of his conduct in his previous existence. Thus every soul is at a different stage and may be ready for a primitive religion or an
advanced one. Hinduism accepts many gods as different
manifestations of the Divine. It records many incarnations
of greater gods in lesser gods or even in men. It tolerates
worship of idols or fertility images, permitting both rites of
the crudest sort and spiritual exercises of a very difficult
nature. The Hindu scriptures, which are written in Sanskrit,
a dead language, are several times the length of the Bible and
have accumulated over a long period. They give no coher-
ence to a religion that is tolerant of great contradictions.

During Karamchand's long illness, the Jain priest before
whom Mohan had taken his vow had often come to the house
to recite from the scriptures in a Gujarati translation. But
the epic poetry he had chosen had given Mohan no real
appreciation of the philosophy on which it was based. Now
in England he was introduced to the English translation of a
fine poem that is part of the Hindu collection and is known
as the *Bhagavad-Gita.*

The subject of the *Gita* is a dialogue between the hero Arjuna and his charioteer, who is a divine being, an incarnation
of the god Krishna. A great battle is impending against the
kindred of Arjuna, who have wronged him. When he sees
the enemy forces assemble and recognizes his close relatives
among them, Arjuna wants to avoid the conflict, even at
the price of submission. The god-charioteer reproves him.
Battle is his duty, and each man must do the thing for which
he is set on earth.

The poem now becomes a lesson on the duty of man, which
is to do right in a selfless spirit above reward or even success.
The man of true spiritual power rises superior to pride, fear,
ambition, love of friends or family, in short to everything that

can attach him to this life. Gandhi drank all this in, but the lesson of the *Gita* which made the strongest impression on him was that a man need not seek spiritual advancement by retiring to a mountaintop or quitting the world. On the contrary, the good man should be a man of action, living in the midst of the world but without being linked to it by any emotional ties, such as personal fears or desires.

It is interesting that this poem, which expressed such deep spiritual truths to the future apostle of nonviolence, should actually be about the duty of fighting. Gandhi felt free to interpret war in the *Gita* as spiritual combat, but it is possible to read into its argument a defense of violence in a just cause. Many Hindus did so, basing their opposition to Gandhi and his methods on the very poem which had largely inspired him.

The Song Celestial, as the English translation of the *Gita* was called, was less an accurate translation than an adaptation of the poem for an English audience. In other words, it stressed the unity of its thought in a fashion which had not seemed necessary to the original author in a more primitive and less organized age. Like Shelley or Thoreau, to whom the vegetarians had introduced him, it gave Gandhi a modernized exposition of ideas that had been presented to him in India less as philosophy than sanctified family tradition. Thus the discussions into which his vegetarian associates plunged him were perhaps the only ones in London that could have reconciled him to a religion he had questioned since his adolescence, yet to which he was bound by family ties and by the demands of his conscience.

It was only natural that sooner or later someone in England would introduce Mohan to the Bible. With a systematic approach that was already characteristic, he sat down to read it from end to end, only to find much of the Old Testament repulsive and more of it hideously dull. The New Testament

Young Gandhi in European dress

did delight him, especially the Sermon on the Mount. He started going to fashionable churches on a Sunday to listen to the best preachers of the time. On the whole, he found much in Christianity and always retained respect for its moral doctrines. But its exclusiveness repelled him, since he felt there were many ways of approaching God.

Mohan's closer introduction to English life seems to have been responsible for a curious episode. He suddenly found it important to become the complete English gentleman, spent money on a high silk hat and a beautiful suit he could ill afford, patent leather boots, gloves, and a silver-mounted cane. He even wrote to Laxmidas that he needed a watch chain of gold. He found someone to tutor him in French, someone else for elocution. He started dancing classes and bought a violin. But his own extravagance soon appalled him. He could not make his feet follow Western music, which was in any case quite strange to him. He had no gift at all for the violin. He was not by temperament social. His conscience told him that he was wasting his time and also the family money. Soon he went to the other extreme and decided on rigid economy. He moved to a cheaper lodging where he cooked his own breakfast and supper of oatmeal and cocoa. He gave up public transportation and walked everywhere, which he decided was of great benefit to his health. He got a notebook and made a careful list of expenses, entering daily every penny he spent, even down to postage stamps.

His education proceeded in a systematic way. To receive a law degree he had to attend the Inner Temple for three years, proving his presence in London by eating six dinners at the Temple every term. People could and did do other things besides studying during these years; and even allowing for his defective education, Gandhi had spare time. He decided to sit for the London Matriculation Examination, which involved him in French and Latin besides other subjects. This made him work hard, and he set himself to it by the clock, devoting so many hours at a time to Latin, so many to law.

Three years must have been a long, dreary period, made endurable to Gandhi by regimenting himself, marking off little successes in discipline, and developing the habits that would stand him in good stead in later life. He formed no friendships that mattered to him later, but arrived and left a lonely young man. In June 1891, he celebrated his going by giving a farewell dinner for the Vegetarian Society in an expensive restaurant. He was supposed to make a graceful speech on the occasion, but got off to a bad start, stammered nervously, and sat down. Two days later he learned he had passed his examinations. He spent one day on the business necessary for being "called to the bar" as an accredited lawyer. On the second day, he sailed for home.

Lawyer in South Africa

LAXMIDAS, WHO MET his brother in Bombay, brought the news that their mother was dead. It was a bitter blow to Gandhi, for his devotion to Putliba had made him what he was. For her sake he had abstained from wine and women as well as meat. He had cut himself off from convivial evenings with the friends he might have made; he had withdrawn from young women who assumed that at his age he was not married. His whole relationship with English people had been affected by the fact that, though living among them, he could not do what they did. Self-discipline of no ordinary kind had been required. Besides, Mohan's love had been given to his mother without restraint. In his affection for her and only for her there had been no hint of the difficulty that was to vex him in later life, namely, how to reconcile family relationships with love for all, or even with detachment from the world.

It was a bad time for such a loss, for young Gandhi had returned to face serious problems. There was first his defiance of the caste to consider. He made a pilgrimage with

Laxmidas, after which he offered a dinner to the caste elders in Rajkot, humbly serving it stripped to the waist. These measures were only moderately successful. In Rajkot he was readmitted, but not in Bombay or in Porbandar, where he could not so much as take a meal with his father-in-law.

Even harder was the question of his future. Rajkot and Porbandar had plenty of lawyers. Bombay was dominated by a closed group, unlikely to open their ranks to a stranger, especially one at odds with his own caste. Even when Gandhi applied to a school for a post as teacher of English, he was turned down for lack of a B.A.

He did stay in Rajkot for a while doing odd jobs for his brother; but his pride was bitterly hurt. Perhaps to assert himself, he made life difficult for his family, insisting that they wear European clothes, eat oatmeal, and drink cocoa. Kasturbai must learn to read and write, use a knife and fork, and acquire English social graces. He raged at her for her failures and eventually sent her back for a time to her father.

He himself departed for Bombay, hoping at least to gain knowledge of Indian law, of which his education had left him ignorant. But his first and only appearance in court was a failure because of stage fright. He returned his client's fee and went despairingly back to Rajkot, where he busied himself working up briefs for other lawyers.

Laxmidas, it appeared, had badly misjudged the situation in sending Mohan to London. Perhaps if he himself had risen to his father's position, he might have been able to smooth the way for his younger brother. Laxmidas had started out well enough by obtaining through his uncle the position of secretary and adviser to the Prince of Porbandar. This young man, before he inherited the throne, removed some of the crown jewels from the state treasury. The British agent, a Mr. Ollivant, whose job it was to prevent the local princes from converting state funds to their private needs, was informed that the Prince had acted on the advice of Laxmidas. He therefore saw to it that the secretary was dismissed.

It happened that Mohan had been introduced to Mr. Ollivant when the agent was on leave in London. Ollivant had been pleasant to the young student from Rajkot. To Laxmidas, who had grown up among the petty intrigues of a tiny court, it was obvious that Mohan should use this contact as a chance to get his brother reinstated.

Mohan did not take this view, but he owed too much to his brother to refuse. He made an appointment with Mr. Ollivant, but realized from the first greeting that the official behind his desk was very different in manner from the man who had been gracious to him in London. The moment he started on his brother's case, Ollivant cut him off sharply. Laxmidas was an intriguer, and in any case he should present a proper petition if he wanted to justify himself. Conscious of obligation, young Gandhi persisted. Ollivant got up to close the conversation and asked his visitor to leave. Embarrassed but determined, the young man tried a third time. Ollivant called in the doorkeeper, who took him by the shoulders and pushed him out of the room.

This physical assault was one humiliation too many. Young Gandhi threatened suit, but in Rajkot there was no redress to be had. A distinguished Bombay lawyer to whom he turned for advice told him that British officials were all arrogant and that he would have to learn to put up with insult. Mohan was powerless, but his bitterness ran deep. For the first time he felt critical of British rule in India and doubtful of his future in such a land. He felt a stranger in his own country, his native town, even his household. He raged at the pettiness of provincial Rajkot. Laxmidas, earning a modest living drawing up minor legal documents, could help him little; but while Mohan was in this despairing mood, a suggestion came from Porbandar.

Any port, no matter how sleepy, is a window onto the world. Dada Abdulla, shipowner and trader of Durban in South Africa, was a native of Porbandar, where he still had a cousin and partner. This cousin now wrote to Laxmidas, inquiring whether his young brother would care to go to South Africa for a year. Dada Abdulla had interests not merely in Durban, which was the chief port of the British Crown Colony of Natal, but also in Johannesburg, a gold-mining town in the Boer republic of the Transvaal. He had recently become involved in a lawsuit over a large sum of money with another Indian merchant in Johannesburg. South African lawyers were working on the case, but the cousin in Porbandar felt a lawyer of Indian background would be a valuable assistant to them. He offered a first-class return fare and a hundred and five pounds for the year, with all expenses.

To Gandhi, this was a providential offer. It afforded a solution to all his immediate problems, including that of Kasturbai, who had recently borne a second son called Manilal. He may have felt a certain relief in being separated from a wife so insensitive to Western culture. She could stay with Laxmidas, and the hundred pounds would be plenty for her keep. Thus in April 1893, Gandhi set out again on his travels.

Dada Abdulla, who met him on the quay in Durban, was an illiterate, mild-mannered, devout Muslim of great business ability who was one of the leading Indians in the Crown Colony. He did not really want the young lawyer whom his cousin had sent over. He had excellent legal advice on the spot; and the lawsuit would be tried in Pretoria, the capital of the Transvaal, according to Boer law, about which young Gandhi knew nothing. Dada Abdulla gave himself a few days to consider whether he could fit the young man into some minor post. In the meantime, he took him along to court, where he was involved in another case. Young Gandhi was wearing correct and formal English costume, but with a black turban on his head. The magistrate told him to take this off in court.

Sensitive to a possible slight, Gandhi looked around to find other Indians present still wearing their turbans. It did not occur to him that a distinction was being made between Muslim turbans, which by agreement were kept on, and Hindu turbans. Nor did he know that in the eyes of South Africans, Indian immigrants were divided into definite classes. At the top came the Muslim merchants, followed by their clerks, who were mostly Parsees. At the bottom came the mass of Hindus, nearly all laborers from South India, who were called "Sammies" because their names so often ended in "-sami." As a Hindu lawyer, London-trained and taught to consider himself a gentleman in English terms, Gandhi did not fit these classifications. He was, moreover, quick to suspect insult. Coldly replying that he had no intention of removing his turban, he walked out of the court. He returned to Dada Abdulla's and wrote a letter to the local paper, explaining his action.

This little episode drew the attention of the Indian community in Durban to the stranger in their midst. It began to dawn on Dada Abdulla that the young man had character. A short while later when the merchant was summoned to Pretoria to give evidence in his case, he decided to send Gandhi to represent him, since he could not personally take the time from his business. The young man was extensively briefed, and Dada Abdulla's agents in the towns along his route were all alerted to give him every possible assistance. Then, provided with a first-class ticket and urged by Dada Abdulla to

indulge himself in every reasonable comfort, he set out.
The train from Durban only ran as far as the Transvaal
border, but this in itself was an overnight trip. When they
reached Pietermaritzburg, the capital of Natal Colony, a
European entered Gandhi's compartment, looked him up and
down, and went away to find a railroad official. Presently
a man in uniform ordered Gandhi into the van.

"I have a first-class ticket," he protested, producing it.

The official waved the ticket aside. Sammies belonged in
the van with other natives.

Gandhi refused to move. After an argument, the official
went for a policeman, who removed him by hustling him out
of the compartment onto the platform. His luggage was
thrown off the train, which departed without him.

Gandhi made his way to the waiting room. It was getting
late and the night was cool; but his overcoat was in his luggage, which had been collected by the station officials. He
was too much afraid of further insult to reclaim it. Shivering
with cold, with nervous tension, and with fury, he was
tempted to wipe the dust of South Africa off his feet forever.
Remembering, however, that he had duties to perform for
Dada Abdulla in Pretoria, he determined to remain and put
up a fight against color prejudice, not only for his own sake,
but for that of his fellow Indians. The unknown European,
presumably of Dutch or English extraction, who was now
happily on his way to the Natal border, had started something greater than he had any idea of. Little Mr. Gandhi,
sitting up on a hard station bench in Pietermaritzburg, was
making up his tenacious mind to take on as an opponent
the whole white population of South Africa.

Next morning he sent a telegram of protest to the manager
of the railroad and an explanatory one to Dada Abdulla, who
in his turn entered a protest. The merchant also communi-

cated with Pietermaritzburg, where his agents came to the
station and rescued Gandhi, informing him that such insults
were the regular thing. An entire compartment was reserved
for the rest of his journey, and he proceeded on his way
the following evening.

The train tracks ended in Charlestown on the Natal border,
and he had to go on by coach. It was at once made clear to
him that darkskinned passengers sat outside by the driver.
Since he had to comply or go no farther, he took the outside
seat. As the day wore on, however, it may have been more
pleasant out in the open than inside the stuffy coach. At all
events the Dutchman who acted as guard and took charge of
the passengers decided to ride outside for a change. Throwing a piece of dirty sacking on the footboard, he said to Gandhi, "Sammy, you sit on this. I want to sit near the driver."

Gandhi refused.

The burly Dutchman clouted him over the head and tried
to shove him onto the footboard, knocking him about and
shouting curses at him. Gandhi did not hit back because he
was too busy trying to hold on. Passengers stuck out their
heads and, seeing that he did not retaliate, they shouted to
the Dutchman, "Leave him alone!"

Luckily there was room for three on the seat, and the other
place was occupied by a black servant. The Dutchman ordered this man to sit on the footboard and lowered himself
into the place next to Gandhi. The coach lumbered on, while
now and then the Dutchman would turn to the little Indian by
his side and growl to him, "Just wait till we reach Standerton,"
where the coach stopped for the night. "I'll show you . . ."

At Standerton, Gandhi was relieved to be greeted by more
friends and agents of Dada Abdulla. The Dutchman was unable to make good his threats, and next morning the journey

was resumed in a different coach. On this occasion Gandhi
sat inside, arriving without incident in Johannesburg.

He should have been met here, but there was a hitch. He
drove to a hotel and was turned away. "Sorry," they said
unconvincingly, "full up." He spent the night with another
of his employer's agents.

From Johannesburg to Pretoria there was a railroad, on
which Sammies were supposed to travel third class. However, by applying directly to the stationmaster and impressing
him with his European clothes and fluent English, Gandhi
managed to obtain a first-class ticket. When the guard came
around, he was ordered out of his compartment. Again he
refused, but this time a friendly Englishman who shared it
with him took his part. He arrived at Pretoria without further
trouble, but with his eyes fully opened to the position of
Indians in South African life.

He spent the rest of this year in Pretoria, working on
the case. Mr. Baker, Dada Abdulla's lawyer there, was an
evangelical Christian, saved, as he liked to maintain, by
the blood of Jesus. He had built a church with his own
money and was most anxious to convert young Gandhi.
Gandhi was always interested in religion, even though he was
repelled by Mr. Baker's exclusive brand of salvation and
critical of the lawyer's personal moral values. He was again
challenged to think about his own faith, the more so because
he soon began to take steps toward improving the position
of the Indian community.

Characteristically, he did not start by attacking white
attitudes, but by changing the Indians themselves. He summoned a meeting to tell them of their faults. They had a bad
name in business for lying. Their insanitary habits were often
offensive to westerners. Too few of them bothered to learn

English, the common language even in the Transvaal. Finally, they had no community group, either for self-improvement or to present a united point of view. Indians listened, and one or two asked him for English lessons. It dawned on others that these criticisms were intended to improve their public image. Merchants began to invite the young man to their houses and to give thought to his ideas. They found him persuasive, partly because nobody else had taken the trouble to think about their community standing, or even to treat Muslim, Parsee, and Hindu as parts of one whole.

Meanwhile, in the lawsuit young Gandhi was proving his value. The cousin had been right in sending for him, if only for the reason that most of the correspondence involved was in Gujarati. The remarkable powers of application that Gandhi had developed during his studies in London enabled him to master the complications of a commercial case despite his lack of knowledge of business procedures. Moreover, he soon perceived that court costs would be so great that the result of a lawsuit might well be loss to both claimants. It would be better policy to submit the case for arbitration. He urged this point of view not only on Dada Abdulla, but also on his opponent, demonstrating such good sense that both parties were persuaded by this unknown young man in his early twenties. The arbitration took place and resulted in a complete victory for Dada Abdulla. The loser was threatened with bankruptcy, which in his own eyes and those of his fellow Muslims would be an irredeemable disgrace. Gandhi set himself to persuade Dada Abdulla to take payment of the debt in gradual installments, which would leave his opponent in business. Prevailing, he won the gratitude of both merchants as well as a reconciliation between them. In other words, young Gandhi was beginning to show remark-

able talents, though these had nothing whatever to do with
the showy qualities of a court lawyer.

Dada Abdulla felt greatly obliged to him and honored him
with a big farewell party in Durban before he returned to
India. At this party, somebody handed Gandhi a copy of
The Natal Mercury, in which he happened to notice a brief
paragraph headed THE INDIAN FRANCHISE. A bill was being
presented before the Legislative Assembly of the colony to
deprive Indian residents of the vote.

Dada Abdulla shrugged his shoulders. He had no interest
in any news outside the stock market prices. All the other
merchants agreed there was nothing to be done about any
issue on which the white men of Natal made up their minds.

Gandhi argued. The vote was fundamental to Indian rights
and self-respect. They ought to organize a petition. Well
then, would he stay and lead opposition to the bill? Dada
Abdulla, who had no mind to pay all the expenses of a political campaign, suggested that leading merchants offer Gandhi
an annual retainer to represent their interests in general.
Thus the matter was arranged, and his passage was canceled.

There was an enormous amount to do. Gandhi must
arrange meetings to arouse the Indian community. He must
appeal for campaign funds. He must see government officials,
draw up a petition, and even approach the Colonial Office in
London. He tackled all these tasks with quiet efficiency. His
tone to Indians and Englishmen alike was reasonable, never
angry. His arguments were sound and legalistic, not emotional, though capable of arousing emotion in others. No one
ever seemed less like an agitator than he, even while his house
and his office were crowded by volunteers collecting signatures, addressing envelopes, and helping where they could.
His petition to the Assembly was presented in little over a

month, though he had taken time to marshal opinions against the bill in masterly detail.

The vegetarians and the Indians of Durban may perhaps occasionally have noticed that the shy, almost retiring Gandhi had power over men. He now proved capable, when his interest was aroused, of unending persistence and untiring industry. Nothing was left undone for lack of time; nothing was forgotten or untried. His approach to everyone was the same. His cause was righteous, as he was prepared to prove by argument. He thought that anyone he could convince was bound to support him, because he believed that men are good by nature and do what is good if they really understand it. It naturally followed that if Gandhi failed to convince, the fault was in him. This sweetly reasonable point of view was usually disarming and won him friends in high places among the Europeans of Natal. It was hard not to like him, more especially as, despite his earnestness, there was persistently a twinkle in his eye.

It soon became clear that the cause Gandhi had undertaken to defend was not merely that of the Indian vote but that of the very existence of the Indian community in Natal. Most Indians in South Africa had been imported as indentured laborers, temporary slaves in mines or on plantations, who had simply stayed on after their time of service ran out. They were and usually remained exceedingly poor. The colony now proposed to tax these men twenty-five pounds, far more than they could possibly pay, in order to find an excuse for dumping them back again in India, where they had little prospect of getting work.

Gandhi fought this threat by every means. He appealed to the Viceroy of India, to the Colonial Secretary in London, to Naoroji, the Indian member of Parliament who was at this time educating Mohammed Ali Jinnah in English politics. He wrote articles; he made speeches; he even registered as an advocate before the Supreme Court of Natal, and for the purpose consented to remove his turban in court.

Considering that the white inhabitants of Natal were generally determined to destroy the Indian community, Gandhi's campaign was remarkably successful. He did not win the vote for Indian immigrants, but he succeeded in retaining those who were already on the voting lists. Similarly he did not get the tax abolished, but he did reduce it to a poll tax of three pounds, a heavy burden, but payable at least by some. A still more important achievement was the creation of an Indian organization called the Natal Indian Congress in imitation of the Indian Congress, meeting place of India's nationalist leaders. But the Natal Indian Congress was very much Gandhi's own creation and had two important differences from its original. In the first place it was no biennial conference, but a permanent organization supported by dues-paying members and containing an education branch in which young Indians could learn to debate current issues. In the second place, Gandhi's legal services were extended freely to the poor, so that the name of the congress that he represented soon came to be known not merely to the wealthy elite, but to the masses. Meanwhile, as part of his mission, Gandhi never ceased to urge his fellow Indians to learn English and put into practice those ideals of self-improvement that he had begun to develop in Pretoria. Thus by 1896 when he decided to revisit India, he had behind him an organized group whose needs and views he meant to present to Indian nationalists. It was time to do so, and time also to think of Kasturbai and his two sons, who had been with Laxmidas for three years.

The Green Book

GANDHI SAILED for India in June 1896, using his leisure on the voyage to commence a booklet prosaically entitled: *The Grievances of the British Indians in South Africa, An Appeal to the Indian Public*. Published in Rajkot with a green cover, it came to be generally known as "The Green Book." The tone of his argument was reasonable, and an English newspaper in Bombay gave it favorable notice. Unfortunately Reuters news agency created an uproar in Durban by a cable quoting Gandhi as saying that Natal Indians were "robbed, assaulted and treated like beasts." For this piece of imagination, Gandhi was to pay dearly.

He spent five months in India, during which he traveled extensively, seeing much of the land for the first time and meeting important Indians who might be useful to his cause. In particular, he made acquaintance with Tilak and Gokhale, two Indian nationalists who were in their different ways the founding fathers of the independence movement.

Tilak, who was at this time about forty years old, repre-

sented the extreme, even violent tendencies of Indian nationalism. A gifted educator and newspaperman, he had built up
the circulation of two papers, one in English and one in his
native tongue, Marathi, and had made them leading organs
of Hindu political thought. Indeed, Tilak had actually introduced Western political concepts into Marathi, inventing
idioms to convey these to his public. His influence on Hinduism in general had been equally creative. The festival of the
elephant-god Ganesh, which had by tradition been a household celebration, had been transformed by Tilak into a ten-
day public affair, featuring not only the processions traditional in Hindu festivals, but also literary and musical contests
accompanied, for the first time in the Hindu world, by political speeches. In other words, Tilak aroused the pride of Hinduism in its own ancestral traditions, associating this with a
demand for political freedom. His position was that of a genuine revolutionary, not afraid of violence. Indeed, in 1896, he
was already caught up in a crisis that would lead to his trial
in the following year for incitement to political murder.

Violence was alien to Gandhi, but he found much to admire
in Tilak, especially his love for Hindu tradition and his appeal
to national pride. After Tilak's death Gandhi was to move
gradually closer to Tilak's position, offering not precisely violence, but a method that sometimes appeared to his British
opponents very much like it. This, however, lay years ahead;
at the moment, he felt personally and politically closer to
Gokhale.

Gandhi always felt that he was in a certain sense Gokhale's
disciple. As he himself would explain, he never met anyone
to whom his spirit paid absolute homage. Nevertheless, from
the moment the two met, Gokhale represented to him the
ideal Indian politician.

Gokhale was a moderate, seeking progress toward Indian

home rule by peaceful means. The British never thought Gokhale dangerous, but they recognized his nobility of soul. Gokhale had also founded a society called The Servants of India, dedicated to social work and to the improvement of the many miseries of India. Compared to Tilak, Gokhale was in touch with Indian life at all levels, recognizing, even if in a limited way, that the mass of Indians was beyond reach of newspapers or ten-day festivals, and that the villages were remote from the sound of nationalist propaganda.

Contacts such as these made young Gandhi friends in powerful places, introducing him to people of greater ability and wider horizons than he was accustomed to meet. In Natal, he stood out precisely because the Indians, who had come to the colony to make themselves a living, were occupied with nothing else. Fundamentally they were simple people to whom the developing genius of Gandhi had been a marvel. In India, the young man neither was nor thought himself the equal of Tilak or Gokhale. To them his attitude was appealing because his deference resulted from a realistic appraisal of his worth.

Much of his time in India was spent in Rajkot, knitting up the bonds of family life. There his abundant energies overflowed into public works, so that we find him helping with local preparations for Queen Victoria's Diamond Jubilee and indulging his lifelong passion for better sanitation by inspecting latrines during a plague epidemic. More important personally were his preparations to take Kasturbai and her children back to Durban.

He had given up trying to teach Kasturbai accomplishments, but he was as determined as ever that she should conform to his pattern. In Durban he was the effective leader of the Indian community. His house was large, but crowded with ten or a dozen assistants who gave him most of their time and in some cases lived with him. To the English community he was "presentable," and his house lay in an English quarter. Since this position was politically important, Kasturbai had to do him credit.

It is hard to tell whether Gandhi was ever sensitive to the fears of Kasturbai, who had never been outside Porbandar and Rajkot. She would have to cross the sea; her husband's associates would not speak Gujarati. He was mingling with Muslims and rubbing shoulders with Hindus of every caste, including people whom Kasturbai herself would be frightened to touch. But a Hindu husband is the law in his own household. Kasturbai knew this, and Gandhi claimed his rights. She would have to do as he said, but she could not make herself like it.

He decided that she should wear the Parsee sari instead of the traditional costume that was sacred in her eyes. It looked better and had more social cachet in Durban. The children were to be dressed as Parsees, too, in knee-length coats and tight trousers instead of the comfortable, floppy Hindu dhoti, a loose loincloth or clumsy divided skirt, which unquestionably lacked style and was associated in the South African mind with laboring "Sammies." Worst of all, they had to throw away their sandals in favor of smelly socks and hard leather shoes. But it was useless to complain. The father whose acquaintance they were now making was a person who cared and always would care intensely about correct costume.

They had a bad voyage, and none of them enjoyed it except, unfairly enough, the indestructible Gandhi, who actually liked storms and a chance of attending to seasick passengers. Everybody seems to have wept and given the ship up for lost; it is hard to tell whether Gandhi's assurances carried conviction.

He had sailed on a ship belonging to Dada Abdulla that

was carrying besides cargo about two hundred and fifty Indian passengers. Some of these were the wives and children, nephews or cousins of men who had made good. In other words, the S.S. *Courland* carried a large percentage of immigrants. This in itself was offensive enough, but the return of Gandhi had unfortunately become general knowledge in Durban. The Reuters telegram about the "Green Book" still rankled; and a furious agitation arose among Europeans, who made up their minds to prevent him and his countrymen from landing. The situation was made worse by the simultaneous arrival of another ship belonging to Dada Abdulla, which brought the number of Indian passengers up to some five hundred.

Unfortunately, during Gandhi's absence, a Colonial Patriotic Union had been founded in Durban, dedicated to expelling Indians from Natal. Like most such organizations, its power really rested on its rowdies; but it was sympathetically regarded by people in high political office, either out of conviction or because they did not want to face a riot. Thus under the pretext that there had been plague in Bombay, elaborate quarantine regulations were enforced on Dada Abdulla's ships. All old clothes had to be burned, all new ones disinfected, bedding destroyed and every corner of the ship scrubbed out. Water and provisions were running low, as these delays consumed almost two weeks; but the authorities were in no hurry to send fresh supplies. When they did so, new fumigations were imposed. Eventually, however, after nearly a month, all pretexts were exhausted; and there was nothing to prevent the passengers from landing. At this point the captain received a letter from the Colonial Patriotic Union, threatening that an attempt to land would be opposed by force and suggesting that the ships return to Bombay. The Natal government would pay return fare.

This was a little further than the government was prepared to go. The attorney general, Harry Escombe, who had been a good friend of Gandhi's until the publication of the "Green Book," came aboard to announce that the passengers might disembark. A large crowd had gathered on the wharf, but Escombe in a sensible address ordered them to disperse in the name of the Queen. They gradually did so, and the disembarkation started.

Escombe had given thought to the problem of landing Gandhi, whose face, he feared, would raise a riot. Kasturbai and the boys duly went ashore and were welcomed by friends; but Escombe persuaded Gandhi himself to wait until dark.

After Escombe had left, Gandhi was visited by a Mr. Laughton, one of Dada Abdulla's legal advisers, who strongly urged him to go ashore by day and face his enemies. Sooner or later Gandhi would have to walk down the streets of Durban, and the government had made no arrangement to protect him when he did. The wisest thing was to face the situation once and for all, and Mr. Laughton offered to accompany him in person. Gandhi agreed because he was too proud a man to like concealment. Thus about five o'clock in the afternoon the two went ashore and ordered a rickshaw.

Immediately some boys began yelling, "Gandhi! Gandhi!" A crowd gathered; and the rickshaw boy, scenting trouble, took to his heels. There was nothing to do but walk.

Pretty soon mud and garbage, mixed with stones and other missiles, were showered on the two men. The crowd came closer, hustling Laughton out of the way and leaving their victim unprotected. Someone struck Gandhi with a riding whip. Someone else knocked off his turban. Gandhi gripped hold of a railing to prevent himself from falling, blood streaming from a cut in his neck. The mob closed in for the kill.

At this moment Mrs. Alexander, wife of the police superintendent, who had happened to be walking down the street, plunged into the fray. Struggling to the side of Gandhi through men who either knew her or at least gave place to a respectable woman in a fury, she reached Gandhi's side and defiantly opened her parasol to protect him. A few police constables, aroused by an excited message, came running up.

Mrs. Alexander took Gandhi by the arm; and protected by her voluminous skirts and the sunshade, he managed to advance, while the constables busied themselves in clearing the way. Luckily it was not far to the house of a merchant called Rustomji, with whom he took refuge. The crowd remained outside and, as night fell, became belligerent. Superintendent Alexander had by this time arrived, but his police force was not equal to restraining the mob, which was by now of considerable size. He put a bench across the front door and stood on it facing the crowd. Failing to calm things down, he led them in singing a verse beginning, "We'll hang old Gandhi on a sour apple tree . . ."

Presently, when everyone was hoarse, he tried again to reason with them.

"What do you want?"

"Gandhi!"

"What will you do with him?"

"Hang him!"

"And if you don't get him?"

"Burn the house down!"

The superintendent pointed out that there were women and children inside. By now he had managed to drag the situation out while policemen who had been admitted through a side door were persuading Gandhi to fall in with their plans for smuggling him away.

Bruised but unshaken, Gandhi still wanted to face the

crowd; but he could not risk the lives of Rustomji and his family. Presently a uniformed policeman somewhat under standard size emerged from a side door in company with a white detective. The two made their way over fences and through alleyways to a warehouse, outside which a carriage was waiting for them. Superintendent Alexander, having got the crowd to admit that they would harm no one but Gandhi, took his life in his hands to explain that their prey had slipped off. Alexander was a highly respected man, and his personality prevailed. He told the rioters that they had been in the wrong and must not turn their anger on him for doing his job. The only thing left for them was to come to their senses and go home.

Reaction set in after a couple of days, but the matter could not end here. Gandhi's relationships, now closely knit, with Indian nationalists had brought his predicament to the notice of the Viceroy of India. London had heard of Gandhi, too; and the colonial secretary of the time was Joseph Chamberlain, far the most able politician to hold that office in many years. When Joe Chamberlain sent a telegram to the government of Natal, demanding explanation of the disgraceful incident, Harry Escombe was forced to summon Gandhi and offer to prosecute his assailants.

The ball was in the hands of Gandhi, who replied that these ignorant men were less at fault than Escombe himself and the Natal government, which had permitted the Colonial Patriotic Union to incite Europeans against the Indians. He offered to write a personal note to Chamberlain, explaining that he did not wish to prosecute. Escombe, who was indeed on the horns of a dilemma, was forced to be grateful.

The incident was closed, but it had outlined Gandhi as the leader of the Natal Indian Congress and a person of whom the official world took notice. He could never again escape from publicity. In a certain sense he did not want to; but on the other hand, his preoccupation with himself, developed in London by his vow to his mother, now grew on him as he strove to be personally worthy of his destiny. A public figure may be admired, but admiration makes demands on a man.

Kasturbai and the children found him hard because he was going through a difficult stage. As his fame grew, his private law practice flourished. He was at liberty to spend as much as he pleased of his handsome income in service to the Indian community. Too much of his time, however, was consumed in a profession that did not satisfy his desire to tackle fundamentals. Meanwhile, as tension grew between British Natal and Boer Transvaal, and the outbreak of the Boer War came visibly nearer, European interest was naturally diverted from persecuting the Indian community. In consequence, it became harder to unite the Indians themselves or to interest them in the self-improvement dear to Gandhi's heart. Events were out of his control and forcing him into a success he did not value. No wonder his temper was quick, especially toward Kasturbai.

She had to conform to his ways, but the difficulties that arose after their long separation might have found more sympathetic treatment. Besides Kasturbai and his sons, Gandhi had brought from India the ten-year-old son of his widowed sister. There was also another baby on the way. In other words, the house was filled to bursting, since a number of his law clerks also lived there. The only bathroom was downstairs, so that chamber pots were provided in the bedrooms, an arrangement that was perfectly familiar to Kasturbai. In Rajkot, however, such vessels were handled by an outcaste sweeper because no caste member might touch them without pollution. When Kasturbai was commanded to clean up after her own family, it must have made her ill to comply; but she did so. Worse was to follow. A new clerk came to lodge in the house, an Indian Christian and therefore strongly taboo. For some reason he did not understand about cleaning his own pot as the other clerks did. Gandhi ordered Kasturbai to do it for him.

This would have been bad enough had the clerk been a Brahman. As it was, Kasturbai was degraded below the unspeakably low. It was unthinkable to refuse her husband, but Gandhi saw her coming down the outside stair into the garden with the pot held at arm's length and tears rolling down her cheeks. He lost his temper and shouted at her that in his house orders were to be obeyed with a cheerful smile.

Kasturbai in her turn lost control and burst out at him, "Keep your house to yourself and let me go!"

Beside himself with fury, Gandhi seized her by the hand and pushed or dragged her down the path with the intention of thrusting her out of the garden gate into the street.

"Have you no sense of shame?" she screamed. "Where am I to go? I have no parents or relatives here to harbor me. Being your wife, you think I must put up with your cuffs and kicks. For heaven's sake behave yourself and shut the gate. Let us not be found making scenes like this."

Gandhi, who describes this scene in his autobiography, appears as much shocked by her conduct as by his own. To do him justice, he had not asked her to perform an act he was not ready to do himself, and indeed often did. Sanitation was a passion with him, and he felt no personal pride or dread of pollution. To be sure, he did not quite like losing his temper and making an ugly public scene. He shut the gate, perceiving that he could not really throw Kasturbai out. For that very reason, he was determined to break her to his will.

His family soon involved him in other problems. Harilal and even Manilal were no longer babies, and there was soon another boy called Ramdas. Remembering his own school days, their father was unalterably opposed to an English education, the only sort to be had in Natal. He tried to find a tutor in Gujarati, but none was available. He was coming around to the view that education was unimportant to being a good man. What had his own done but force him into a profession that he did not really think worthwhile?

The consequence of these thoughts was that Gandhi decided to educate his sons and his nephew himself. There was not much room in his busy day, but the children could accompany him on his fairly long walk to the office, so that he could tell them the things they needed to know. Gandhi had a real love for children and also a gift with them, but these qualities failed him in dealing with his sons. He was always trying to obliterate his personal relationship with them. Though conscious of his special obligation, he did not want to squander more affection on the boys than he did on other children. The consequence naturally was that he gave them less. They learned to regard him with awe rather than love, while he in his turn openly preferred his nephew. Later on they resented their lack of the formal education that had so conspicuously developed their father's talents.

Through such difficulties and mistakes, Gandhi was groping after a better way of life, a simpler existence in which a man could measure his success or failure by performance of definite tasks. With this in mind, he found time for two hours daily in a charitable hospital endowed by his good friend Rustomji. Here he learned much from his contacts with poor Indian laborers, supplementing the knowledge he gained of the rich through his law work.

Simplicity soon began to extend from public service into

his home. The household spent too much money that could be better used. Gandhi bought a book on laundering, practiced himself, and taught Kasturbai. His starched collars were not always properly done; and this caused his fellow lawyers a good deal of amusement at first, but he did not mind it. Presently he began to cut his own hair with the help of a mirror for trimming the back, and friends asked if rats had been nibbling at him.

In 1899, he was still groping in this fashion when the Boers invaded Natal. Gandhi's reaction was to demonstrate loyalty to the British Empire. Strangely enough, love of authority was part of the make-up of this most un-revolutionary freedom fighter. His experiences in Natal had taught him not that the British Empire was evil, but that in the colony its principles had been distorted. To him, the empire enshrined the fundamental concept that all British subjects had equal rights. Its imperfections as a system did not outweigh its ideals in Gandhi's mind.

Anxious not merely to help in person, but to demonstrate Indian loyalty in Natal's hour of need, he offered to recruit an Indian ambulance corps. At first he was rejected, but as the crisis deepened, any offer of aid was welcome. The Boers were far better prepared for war, and not encumbered by army commanders who did not understand South African conditions. It looked as though the whole of Natal might be overrun.

Unlikely though it may appear, Gandhi enjoyed the Boer War. The simplicities of life under discipline suited him, while the human qualities of wounded men were often touchingly apparent to the orderlies who risked their lives to bring them in. Thirty-eight of the ambulance corps, including Gandhi, were awarded the South African War Medal. Nevertheless, as the war dragged toward its end, his thoughts became gloomy. He had hoped that the Indians would earn the gratitude of Natal; but politicians had begun talking of a Union of South Africa, comprising the British colonies of Natal and the Cape, together with the two conquered Boer republics. Boer attitudes toward the Indians had always been cruder than those of the English, and it was obvious that Boer influence would be strong when the new union was formed. Gloomily Gandhi felt that his work in South Africa was doomed to failure. No sooner was the war over than he prepared to return to India.

Friends in Natal protested that they would need his help more than ever, and he was forced to promise that in emergency he would return. Since he was still determined to leave, they showered him with presents, including a gold necklace for Kasturbai and other jewelry worth perhaps a thousand pounds. He told himself he had no right to such things, but in the eyes of Kasturbai a woman's ornaments were a proof of her husband's success and of his regard for her. She wore her gifts proudly, no doubt seeing in them compensation for the ornaments that had been sold to send Mohan to England.

Perceiving that Kasturbai would make difficulty about giving up her treasures, Gandhi approached the subject by getting Harilal and Manilal, now thirteen and eight, to agree with his opinion. Then he came to Kasturbai as representative of the united males of the family, demanding that the jewels be returned.

Poor Kasturbai was outraged, more especially because her husband had turned the boys against her. In vain she protested that she was keeping her ornaments for her daughters-in-law and that her husband had no right to take them away.

"Were they given for your services or for mine?" he demanded sternly.

Kasturbai, who had slaved for him like a servant, felt that she had earned the jewels as much as he. Though she could not resist, she thought that she had been unfairly treated. Unmoved, Gandhi deposited the valuables in a Natal bank as emergency funds for the Natal Indian Congress.

He sailed for Bombay, intending to open a law office there. His life so far had held unfulfilled promise. Though he had fought valiantly for Indian rights, he had wearied of the conflict. Though he had been a successful lawyer, he had not cared for his profession. He was going back to India with no clear goal and nothing ahead of him but the practice of law because it was his trade.

Satyagraha

The Indian National Congress, which Gandhi hurried to attend at the end of 1901, had been founded in 1885 with British encouragement to provide an outlet for Indian political ideas and to acquaint British rulers with Indian suggestions. Lacking power to achieve positive results, it had drifted into opposition, becoming a natural meeting place for people who, debarred from business success by caste tradition or lack of capital, found little outlet for their abilities save in the practice of law, an overcrowded profession. Further than this the Congress had never developed; it still consisted of a semiannual conference dedicated to passing motions that it had no organization to carry out. Such as it was, however, the Indian Congress was looked on as the voice of Indian opinion, there being no other. Gandhi's purpose was to add to its list of meaningless resolutions a vote in favor of the Indian cause in South Africa. Almost equally important was the chance to pursue his acquaintance with Gokhale and learn from him about Indian politics.

The Congress was held in a big tent outside Calcutta, and most of the delegates were housed in local colleges. Despite the presence of India's famous men, the participants were, generally speaking, not impressive. Many of them were ambitious rather than important. Moreover, one of the worst things about the caste system, in which every Hindu had been brought up, was its habit of ranking people on the basis not of what they were, but of what they would condescend to do. The attitude thus learned spread through the whole of life. A delegate would not demean himself by carrying a message, answering a letter, or helping out by casually moving a chair. Worse still, the latrines were beneath the notice of even the young volunteers who helped organize meetings for the sake of hearing and seeing such men as Tilak and Gokhale. Before long, the college latrines were in such dreadful condition that the delegates preferred relieving themselves on the grounds, after the fashion of Indian villagers, who habitually used the countryside, surrounding every hamlet with the stinking residues of its inhabitants.

None of this made sense to Gandhi, who himself cleaned out one of the latrines. Next he went to the Congress office and asked if he could help, to the amazement of the self-important little man who was in charge. In the intervals of answering letters and learning a good deal about the workings of Congress, he developed his friendship with Gokhale, who wanted to advise him in every detail of life. Gandhi responded eagerly; but soon the disciple was questioning the master, politely but persistently measuring Gokhale against his own developing standards of perfection. It says much for Gokhale that he not only came out well from such inquisitions, but also appreciated the motive which lay behind them. From the height of his maturity he did not recognize that he was in the presence of a stronger character and a greater political figure; nevertheless, he was delighted with Gandhi. Even the fiasco of the South African resolution did not shake his faith in him. This was passed as the last piece of business, and Gandhi was given five minutes to speak on it. Never a fluent speaker and still afflicted by stage fright despite his experience in South African courts, he stammered ineffectively for two minutes. When the warning bell that told him he had three minutes left was sounded, he had so far lost his head that he forgot what it meant, broke off abruptly, and sat down.

While he was busy elsewhere, his family was in Rajkot. Presently he joined them, and after some hesitation moved them to Bombay. Here in the middle of the summer Manilal came down with typhoid. The doctor who was treating him, alarmed by his loss of strength, prescribed sustaining chicken broth and milk and eggs.

Gandhi was appalled at the suggestion. In South Africa, he had kept up correspondence with the London Vegetarian Society and found a little time for propaganda. He was not precisely prepared to sacrifice his child for his principles, but he convinced himself that he could save both. He took over the nursing and prescribed a three-day fast, interrupted only by sips of orange juice and water. It did no good; the child was eaten up with fever and lost more strength than ever. He seemed to be dying.

Gandhi lay down beside him one night in despair, racking his brains for what he could do. Suddenly he thought of the answer — a wet sheet-pack. Springing up, he wetted a sheet, wrapped it around the boy, and covered him with blankets. Then, leaving Kasturbai in charge, he walked out, unable to watch the result of his experiment. When he came back, the fever had broken, and the child was perspiring normally. His life was saved.

This episode had a peculiar effect on Gandhi, who had always had a passion for nursing other people, whether sea-sick passengers, wounded soldiers, or the sick coolies of Rustomji's hospital. He had, of course, no medical training save that of orderly, which must have included elementary first aid. He had developed, however, strong views on diet and on the importance of fasting to purify the body, clean it out, and give it a rest. Meditation on God was important, too, not because it might move the Almighty to perform a miracle, but because it brought the mind and with it the body back into tune. In accordance with these views, now fortified, he imposed on Manilal forty days of orange juice and diluted milk, accompanying them by spiritual lessons.

Gandhi was essentially a practical man, and the boy's recovery convinced him that his mystical approach to healing had more to recommend it than the mere scientific learning of Western doctors. Increasingly he gave way to his earnest desire to serve the sick by recommending his methods far and wide. He also indulged in experiments on his own diet in the hope of reducing it to basic healthfulness. These tendencies in the end grew so strong that Gandhi's dedication to healing of body and mind took second place only to his great ideal of a free India, purged of the faults of Hindu tradition as well as of the contamination of the West.

He made a fair start with his law practice in Bombay. Gokhale helped him; and it appeared he might look forward to a moderate rather than a distinguished career, when he received a telegram forwarded from Rajkot. It came from Durban. COMMITTEE REQUESTS FULFILL PROMISE. He was summoned back to cope with an emergency and went in a hurry, leaving his family behind to follow later.

In postwar South Africa there was less room for Indians

than ever. As indentured laborers they were still welcome, because native Africans would only work for long enough to get money to buy a wife or have a spree when they got home. But Indians whose indentures had run out, or the shopkeepers and traders who catered to their needs were unwelcome. Moreover, now that British and Boer were soon to be united in the Union of South Africa, the British party was not inspired to annoy the Boers by asserting the rights of all its citizens, even including Indians. The general effect of the war appeared to be that white people were turning against the Indians everywhere. To make matters harder, Gandhi's propaganda on their behalf was no longer useful. He had tried to get Indians to improve their business methods and personal habits, to develop loyalties toward the colony. This had been acceptable to Natal under threat of war; but after victory, it was the Indians' successes that produced ill will and not their failures. The more reasonably Gandhi pointed out their merits, the more deeply he aroused white people's envy. Even Joseph Chamberlain, who visited South Africa at this time, had little attention for Gandhi, who presented him with a petition from the Indians of Natal. The British problem was to assimilate Boers, not to offend them by favors to the Indian group. Gandhi wanted to present another petition in the Transvaal, but he was excluded from the deputation and politely informed that he was not acceptable in government circles. Luckily he had friends enough in important places to be licensed to practice before the Supreme Court in Johannesburg, where he settled down to defend Indian rights.

Curiously enough, the growing intolerance of whites in general had the effect of forcing into Gandhi's arms a few eccentrics with a deep sense of justice. His first stenographer in Johannesburg was a Scotch girl, to whom he was soon referring as his daughter. When she got married, he replaced her with a Russian Jewess, Sonja Schlesin, passionate and difficult, but devoted to Gandhi's cause with all her heart.

Sonja Schlesin, being a Jewess, was naturally concerned with racial tolerance. Walter Rich, who became Gandhi's law clerk, was a Theosophist and as such interested in Indian culture. Albert West, a printer, was a vegetarian who met Gandhi in a vegetarian restaurant. They got to talking and liked one another, but presently Gandhi ceased to appear. Plague had broken out in Johannesburg, and Indian mine workers had been stricken. Gandhi converted an empty store into a temporary hospital, found a better place when it got crowded, discovered a nurse at the Johannesburg General Hospital who was willing to work with plague patients, and persuaded Indians to donate bedding and other necessities. Albert West, who had made inquiries after Gandhi and discovered what he was doing, now offered help. He was without dependents and wanted to serve his fellow men.

Like all great servants of a cause, Gandhi was a dangerous man to approach in such a fashion, for he thought nothing of rearranging other lives to suit his needs. He did not require a European to nurse the Indians, but he wanted desperately a manager with some experience of printing to take charge of *Indian Opinion*, a weekly newspaper he had started in Durban, and was having printed in Gujarati, Hindi, Tamil and English. The very next day, Albert West was leaving for Durban, while Gandhi closed his printing shop and wound up his affairs.

Henry Polak was a vegetarian, too, a Jew, and by profession a newspaper man. He also frequented the vegetarian restaurant and had read with sympathy a letter of Gandhi's to the papers, accusing the authorities of not making proper provision for plague-stricken Indian laborers. He, too, made friends with the little Indian, and they were soon discussing books and ideas.

When Albert West took charge of *Indian Opinion,* he discovered that its affairs were in confusion. Debts were unpaid, accounts ill-kept; it seemed unlikely that the enterprise would ever make a profit, or even that the resources of Gandhi could support it. Gandhi decided to go to Durban in person and discuss what should be done. Henry Polak saw him off, pressing into his hand a copy of John Ruskin's *Unto This Last* to read on the journey.

Unto This Last, though no more than a series of articles combined into a short book, is ambitious reading. It is Ruskin's criticism of the economic and business world of nineteenth-century England. Briefly, his point is that human relationships are more important than economic ones. It is the "invisible gold" of human interest or "social affection" which matters to employer and employed, not the money which passes between them. Ruskin went on to demand that the wealthy regard themselves as servants of the poor, placing themselves in the hands of the community. Following this line of argument, he came around more or less to socialism, community ownership.

It was characteristic of Gandhi that he read books for what he could get out of them, not necessarily for all that the author intended to put in. The organization of industrial society was of little interest to him. The message of Ruskin as he summed it up to himself was threefold. First: the good of the individual is contained in the good of all, or putting it more simply, a man serves his own true interests by serving his community. Second: the work of a lawyer and a barber have the same value because all useful work has the same value. Third: the life worth living is that of the man who works with his own hands. In fact, what Gandhi saw in this book was the development of thoughts over which he was already brooding. He had long been aware, he reflected, that the first principle was true. In a dim way he had appreciated the second. The third had not occurred to him before, yet was it not the answer to his own demands on himself for simplification? How could it be reconciled with the life to which he was committed?

Brim full of new ideas, he burst into the office of *Indian Opinion,* where Albert West was wax in his hands. The press should become a village industry. Its workers should grow their own food, and do their own chores, each be paid an identical wage no matter what his qualifications. Recollections of other communities that had impressed him gave him further ideas. Not far from Durban some Gandhi cousins were settled; and he felt sure he could persuade them to join the experiment. It only remained to find a suitable piece of land near Durban and close to a railway line for the sake of *Indian Opinion.* This was soon discovered at a place called Phoenix, where Gandhi bought eighty acres of fine, fertile soil, including a small orchard.

Gandhi fell on the Phoenix project with enthusiasm. Rustomji and other wealthy friends sent building materials or provided other supplies. Veterans of the ambulance corps volunteered to help with the building. The compositors and staff of *Indian Opinion* moved in, sheltered under canvas until roads, huts and a school could be constructed. There was some objection to the snakes, which were plentiful, but Gandhi made light of such fears. Snakes, he said, were well-disposed creatures who would not bite if one took proper precautions.

Pretty soon the press was set up in an orderly fashion that owed much to Gandhi's inspiration. The settlement itself was like a new toy. He was fascinated by the chance to dominate, strictly for their own good, so many lives. He could not live at Phoenix himself, since his law practice in Johannesburg and his work for Indians there required his presence. But he did import his cousins, and pretty soon brought over from India his eldest son, Harilal, and his nephew Gokuldas. Kasturbai and the younger children were sent there from time to time. Whenever Gandhi had a moment, he would descend on Phoenix, very much the leader and moving spirit of the whole. Henry Polak and Albert West, now completely dominated by him, were encouraged to find suitable wives; and both soon did so. Polak's wife was immediately drafted as governess to Gandhi's younger children, who had joined him in 1905 with Kasturbai. She taught them English, reading, writing and arithmetic, wondering sometimes how they picked up any knowledge whatsoever. Gandhi had by now four sons: Harilal, Manilal, Ramdas and Devadas.

Once more, Gandhi was making a comfortable income, while suffering from inward frustration. His efforts to help the Indians were achieving nothing. His return to South Africa had merely benefited his legal career. Even *Indian Opinion* was having little effect, for Gandhi's compatriots were just as set in their ways as if he had never urged them to change. What use was a group of forty or fifty disciples, including his law clerks and the settlers at Phoenix Farm? It was his ambition to do far more for the human race than this — and time was going past; he was getting close to forty.

He was ripe for a change when the Zulu of Natal rose in rebellion. During all his years in South Africa, Gandhi had taken little interest in the plight of the natives. His time and ideas were fully occupied; and he had never encountered

Africans in their own villages or thought to study native culture. Entrusting his law business to his trained staff and transferring his family to Phoenix Farm, he hurried to Durban to put himself once more at the government's disposal.

He was anxious that Indians should volunteer, not only for ambulance service but also for fighting. By sharing the risks that white men ran, they would win gratitude and respect. For his own part, he raised another small ambulance unit that he commanded with the rank of sergeant major.

He found this war disillusioning because the Zulu were mostly not warriors, but peasant families rounded up into stockades and too often maltreated by the troops. No other ambulance unit would care for Zulu, so that Gandhi's Indians found themselves tending these unfortunate victims to the accompaniment of the jeers of the soldiers. It is true that the campaign was not always brutalizing. There were long and perilous marches, during which respect and understanding grew between the soldiers and the Indians who marched with them. But on arrival at a suspected village, the floggings and arrests began once more.

Inwardly during this campaign Gandhi was making up his mind to a momentous decision that marked a milestone in his private life. Reluctantly chained to his legal practice by the responsibilities of the head of a family, he did not want more children. But he was highly sexed and had been used to indulgence since he was thirteen years old. He abhorred contraceptives, not so much for religious reasons as because they allowed a man to have things both ways. Either it was right to indulge oneself, or it was not.

For a long time he had been trying to avoid Kasturbai, deliberately working himself to the point of exhaustion before sleep. Such methods had not entirely succeeded, and little Devadas was now an extra burden on a man who felt that his energies were needed for community service. Gandhi was thinking over his long abstinence in London as a result of his vow to his mother. That had worked. Why should he not persuade Kasturbai to join him in a vow to live ever after as brother and sister, giving up sex for life? It was good Hindu practice; indeed the ideal Hindu life was divided into stages, the last of which, coming after fatherhood, was that of withdrawal from the world. Many a man who had raised a family would go on pilgrimage, become a monk, or in some other fashion shake off the bondage of this life in hope of bettering his lot in the next incarnation.

What Kasturbai thought about this proposition she kept to herself, agreeing obediently as a Hindu wife must do. The vow, when taken, seemed to alter Gandhi's attitude to her. To his sister, he was not so demanding as to his wife. Kasturbai was free of his rages. On the other hand, he was in a very real sense freed from her. Kasturbai was always with him, a faithful attendant, almost a servant, a faded little peasant woman whose affections were centered on her sons and their descendants. She had to share her husband with other women who were also his "sisters" or his "daughters," who by education were far more fitted to understand and help his work. It was surely hard to be married to a man who reached out to embrace all India in his love, but Kasturbai bore it.

In Gandhi himself, this resolution released new energies. In considering its nature, we need not dwell on psychological factors, such as the guilt produced by the death of his father. Gandhi was no psychiatrist, and it was the practical good that he experienced which interested him. After giving up his most intimate self-indulgence in order to work harder for others, he felt entirely committed to service. What was more, the change involved an inner reorientation. If he was not to be always yearning for the forbidden, he had to direct his energies and desires outward. He had to forget self and find all satisfaction in the good of other people. From this time on, he preached with full conviction that the dedicated life must be a celibate one.

Outwardly, things in Johannesburg were just as before. There was little to show that Gandhi's long apprenticeship was over, that his character had been formed and a close-knit band of workers recruited. But the tempo of events was quickening. Only a month or two after the Zulu rebellion, a measure was introduced into the Transvaal Assembly that was deliberately aimed at Indians.

The Asiatic Law Amendment Ordinance was part of a concerted effort to prevent further Indian immigration into the Transvaal. Conditions being what they were and the Indian community being divided from European settlers by language, residence, customs and religion, it was almost impossible to keep check on its growth. To do so, the new ordinance provided that resident Indians over eight years of age must be fingerprinted and carry a registration card at all times. Not only must this be produced on almost every occasion, but policemen were empowered to enter Indian houses without warrant and arrest anyone who did not have a card. In this fashion, new arrivals who had been smuggled in could be detected.

In these card-carrying days it may be difficult to realize what this ordinance meant to the Indian community; but the experiences of the Jews under Hitler have demonstrated how easy it is for a dominant race to persecute people who have been catalogued in this way. For the moment, the ordinance only applied to the Transvaal; but the danger certainly was that it would be copied by the Orange Free State and thereafter by Cape Colony and Natal. Once registered and counted, Indians could easily be further restricted and eventually forced out of Africa altogether.

Gandhi lost no time in debating with Indian leaders in Johannesburg the implications of this ordinance. Thoroughly aroused, the Indians decided to hold a mass meeting in the Empire Theatre on the afternoon of September 11, 1906, a historic occasion. The Indian community in the Transvaal was perhaps fifteen thousand at this time. Gandhi's work had by now shown even ignorant people that governmental issues were important. The consequence was that three thousand Indians crowded the theater, while hundreds more stood outside. On the platform sat the most influential businessmen of the community.

The chairman, Abdul Gani, who was also chairman of the Transvaal British Indian Association, sounded the note that was to be echoed through the twenty speeches that were given in various Indian languages. He would not register, and if necessary he would go to jail for refusing. Seth Haji Habib went even further and demanded that all the Indians in the Transvaal take a solemn pledge that they would not be fingerprinted or carry cards, no matter what happened.

Gandhi, who had of course arranged the meeting, sat listening to this impassioned oratory punctuated by the cheers of the audience. He was to speak last and sum up the whole, but in the meantime he was pondering over what Seth Haji Habib had said. Fresh from his own vow of celibacy, he was impressed by the sanctity of vows and the realization that they could not be too lightly undertaken. How many of the audience envisaged what might happen if they refused to comply with the law? When his turn came, he tried to make things clear. He personally was willing to take such a pledge and would die rather than break it. Would others do the same?

"We may have to go to jail, where we may be insulted. We may have to go hungry and suffer extreme heat or cold. Hard labor may be imposed upon us. We may be flogged by rude warders. We may be fined heavily and our property may be attached and held up to auction if there are only a few resisters left. Opulent today, we may be reduced to abject poverty tomorrow. We may be deported. Suffering from starvation and similar hardships in jail, some of us may fall ill and die." All this and more might happen; and before taking a solemn pledge, it was only right to face the worst.

He had sounded the right note. With a solemnity that was more impressive than the wild enthusiasm that had greeted earlier speakers, the entire audience rose to pledge themselves to disobedience. A few hours later the Empire Theatre caught fire and burned to the ground, as though it had no further reason for existence after witnessing the birth of civil disobedience in the twentieth century.

So new was the idea that the originator of the movement did not know what to call it. "Passive Resistance," which was the only name which suggested itself, was a poor, negative term for a rallying cry. Gandhi sponsored a contest in *Indian Opinion* to name the new movement; and Manganlal Gandhi, one of his cousins, suggested "Firmness in a Good Cause" or "Sadagraha." Gandhi liked the general idea but soon transformed it into *Satyagraha,* which can best be translated as "Truth Force." The passive resister acts solely because he is right, so that Truth is his only Force. This concept never passed into the English language, so that we have had to make do with clumsy phrases like "civil disobedience" or "nonviolent noncooperation." Perhaps partly for this reason, these terms have frequently been applied to movements which would never have come under Gandhi's definition of *Satyagraha.*

The Nonviolent War

MARTYRDOM WAS NOT called for immediately, for the ordinance was not yet law. It was certainly going to pass in the Assembly, but the Colonial Secretary in London had power of veto. The Colonial Secretary at this time was Lord Elgin, an ex-viceroy of India, who might be expected to understand the Indian view. Less than a month after the Empire Theatre meeting, Gandhi was on his way to London. Here, in a masterly campaign carried out within forty days he acquainted Parliament with the issue and assembled a distinguished group to aid him in putting his points to Lord Elgin. He led a second deputation to the Secretary of State for India to ask for a Royal Commission to inquire into Indian grievances in South Africa. He even sought an interview with the Undersecretary of State for the Colonies, Winston Churchill, Britain's youngest rising politician, who had fought in the Boer War and served in the Indian army. Unsympathetically, Churchill pointed out that even if Lord Elgin were to veto the law, the Transvaal was due to become self-governing in January 1907, and would be able to pass whatever laws it pleased.

This was well known to Gandhi, but he was hopeful that the disapproval of the Colonial Office would discourage the Transvaal from pushing the matter further. But though he was successful in obtaining Elgin's veto, the law was passed again in March 1907 and put into force on the first of July. It was time for the application of *Satyagraha*.

The techniques of mass disobedience had all to be invented. Perceiving that violence would destroy the moral effect at which he was aiming, Gandhi organized his forces carefully. Registration offices were surrounded by pickets, instructed to hand out pamphlets and to reason with Indians going in to register. The names of those who persisted were published in *Indian Opinion* under the heading of "Blacklegs." Each group of pickets was put under command of a captain responsible for its behavior and reporting to a command post, which in turn reported to Gandhi. Many of the pickets, however, were boys in their teens whose self-control was not to be relied on. The Indian community was soon divided by feuding over such violence as did arise, but only about five hundred dared to register. Meanwhile, the streets were plastered with posters written by Gandhi, proclaiming BOYCOTT, and explaining:

> By Going to Gaol we do not resist, but
> suffer for our common good and self-respect.

The "Black Act," as the Indians by now called it, provided that any Indian still without a card after the end of July could be deported. As Gandhi explained to his followers, a man would not actually be hustled out of the Transvaal by force, but served with a deportation order and jailed if he remained. If Indians stood firm, jails would soon be overflowing, and the government would not be able to carry sentences out.

Reluctant to face determined opposition, the government extended the time of registration, first through August, then through September, October and November. These concessions merely encouraged Gandhi's workers. Forced into a trial of strength, the government finally arrested a Hindu priest called Ram Sundara, one of Gandhi's picket captains, who had entered the Transvaal under a temporary permit, now expired. Gandhi defended him in court by admitting the truth of the accusation and justifying it as obedience to a higher law. Ram Sundara was duly sentenced to a month in jail, while Gandhi dramatized the occasion by sending telegrams of protest to the King and the Viceroy of India, closing all Indian stores for a day of mourning, and proclaiming Ram Sundara as a Hindu religious martyr. Meanwhile, the government, uncertain how to handle the matter, allowed Ram Sundara a separate cell in jail and gave him permission to receive visitors, all of whom he lectured about the importance of defying those laws which conflict with a man's conscience. Released when his month was up, he was taken in procession through the Indian quarter, presented with addresses of welcome, and garlanded with flowers. At his elbow was Gandhi, drafting prudent letters or speeches, for the priest was a volatile person, overexcited by notice. The temple that he served had been empty during his absence, and vandals had left it in a deplorable condition. Gandhi stage-managed a lengthy protest to the government for interfering with Hindu religious functions.

At this point, the government served Ram Sundara with a deportation order, threatening more drastic proceedings unless he left the Transvaal. They had judged their man only too well. Ram Sundara had a family to support and was not the sort of man that martyrs are made of. Perceiving that the government really meant business, he departed for Natal. Gandhi was left to attack with venom in *Indian Opinion* the very man whom he had just held up as a hero.

If this was round one, the government had certainly scored. It was now emboldened to attack the real fomenter of trouble. Early in January 1908, Gandhi was brought to court for failure to register. He admitted the fact and asked for the severest penalty of the law, namely six months' imprisonment at hard labor and a fine of five hundred pounds. Taken aback by this approach, the magistrate sentenced him to two months' imprisonment without hard labor.

It was the first of many jail sentences and for that reason the hardest to face. How could Gandhi be certain that the whole campaign would not collapse without him? How would he be treated now that his enemies had him in their hands? He maintained his composure only with an effort; but though the government was not making the mistake it had made with Ram Sundara, its treatment of Gandhi was coldly correct. Prison sanitation, he was pleased to find, was decent; but the worn clothes he was given were degrading, and furniture was simply a plank bed. He had made up his mind to be a model prisoner, but this did not prevent him from objecting to the food which, designed for Kaffir prisoners, gave Indians indigestion. Presently he gained permission for himself and those who had joined him in prison to cook their own food.

Meanwhile, the editor of the Johannesburg daily paper, an old acquaintance of Gandhi's, offered his services to the government as mediator. Several secret meetings took place in the jail; and a general agreement was hammered out, providing that details in the Black Act that had offended Indian sensibilities should be altered, but that the Indians should agree to register. It was suggested, rather than promised, that once the government had saved face, the law could be repealed.

These negotiations were carried on with the connivance of General Smuts, the Boer War hero who was long to remain the dominant figure in South African politics. The agreement was finally signed in a top-secret meeting with Smuts that was arranged like a piece of cloak-and-dagger fiction. Gandhi was taken from his cell on pretext of seeing the superintendent, changed in his office into civilian clothes, and was driven in a closed automobile to the nearest railroad station, where he was hustled into a reserved compartment with the blinds drawn. He was told to occupy himself with reading and not to show surprise when the train was halted a few miles from Pretoria terminal. He was put into another car and driven to the Colonial Office, where Smuts was waiting to see him.

To have forced this meeting on Smuts was an extraordinary triumph for Gandhi, but the agreement to which he consented was a surrender. Gandhi was not fighting for unrestricted Indian immigration, but for the rights of those already in the Transvaal. He was forced to admit the logic of Smuts's argument that no check could be made on Indian numbers without some form of registration. Thus he consented to urge his fellow Indians to cooperate, provided that they were not coerced. The effect was that the government won the second round, for Smuts did not consider his undertaking to work for repeal of the law as really binding. When he found that, as he had expected, the leaders of the Assembly were adamant, he felt himself absolved from further action. Thus in response to a pledge of voluntary registration, Gandhi had gained nothing but modification of minor details.

He found out his mistake immediately. It had been in his

power to summon men to endure jail, ruin, or even loss of life. Having done so, however, he could not decently emerge from jail before his sentence was up, to call for surrender. The story got about that he had accepted a bribe; and though no one who knew him could believe this, the rumor did damage.

Conscientiously Gandhi tried to persuade his followers and determined to set an example by registering on the first day that the offices were reopened for the purpose. On his way there, accompanied by a few friends, he was accosted by a group of Pathans, headed by a six-foot fellow whom he knew well and who now demanded with an unfriendly intonation, "Where are you going?"

"I am going to take out a registration certificate," retorted Gandhi calmly, passing him as he added an invitation to come along.

The Pathan lifted a club and struck him from behind,

General Jan Christian Smuts, dominant figure in South African politics

though luckily the blow missed the back of his neck and landed across his half-turned face. He cried out to God, as the pious Hindu hopes to do at the moment of death, and fell, striking his head against a jagged stone. The men closed in on him, beating, kicking and scuffling with the friends who attempted a rescue. Police ran up and scattered the combatants, finding Gandhi unconscious in a pool of blood. They carried him into a nearby shop, where he recovered sufficiently to insist that the registrar be summoned to take his fingerprints.

It was a good while before he recovered, for his injuries were serious. Eventually he was able to travel to Durban in order to explain to his followers there his agreement with Smuts. This meeting broke up in a riot as someone stormed the platform, club in hand, while someone else fired a blank shot from a revolver. Superintendent Alexander, still in office, thought the situation serious enough to give Gandhi a bodyguard.

His position was saved by the government's refusal to repeal the registration law. Evidently Gandhi had expected Smuts to conduct a public campaign against it, and he was quick to accuse him of lack of good faith. He staged the burning of registration cards in a dramatic meeting and made preparations to resume the struggle.

Warned by the cautious tactics of the government, which had up to now confined its arrests to a few leaders, Gandhi decided to cause confusion by filling the jails through defiance of some other simple law as an act of protest. It was agreed that the easiest way to get arrested was for Indians to sell goods in the streets as unlicensed hawkers, embarrassing authority by their sheer numbers.

This was an activity in which Gandhi did not join, for it might lead to forfeiture of his position as a licensed attorney, which was important to the success of court proceedings. In his place, he threw his twenty-year-old son Harilal into the fray, explaining in *Indian Opinion* that whatever his son did at his own instance might be taken to have been done by himself in person.

A sensitive youth, Harilal had never been highly regarded by his father, who diagnosed a strain of weakness in him. Gandhi blamed himself for this failing because Harilal had been conceived during his father's adolescence and was, for this reason, a child of lust and sin. But instead of regarding the boy with extra tenderness because of his own fault, Gandhi was easily tempted to consider him hopeless from birth. Meanwhile, Harilal, who was probably the most intelligent of Gandhi's sons, yearned for the higher education that his father thought likely to corrupt him further. Some compromises had been reached, and about two years earlier Harilal had been in India, where he had boarded in the household of a well-known Kathiawar lawyer.

How much education he received there is uncertain, but he fell in love with the lawyer's daughter Gulab; and greatly to Gandhi's disgust, he married her. Gandhi's dislike of early marriages was by now reinforced by the conviction that a really good man ought never to have time for marriage at all. It was clear to him that Harilal was indulging the baser side of a weak nature, and it was only with difficulty that he could be brought to accept a daughter-in-law who was charming, virtuous, deeply in love, and the daughter of a friend.

In these circumstances, Gandhi undoubtedly thought he was doing the best for his son by throwing him bodily into the struggle against the Black Act. The unhappy young man, still dependent on his father, was morally bullied into courting jail and breaking the law again as soon as he was released. One way and another, he spent over a year in prison, worrying desperately about his wife alone amid strangers at Phoenix Farm, already nursing one baby with another on the way. Meanwhile, Gandhi himself was cheering up Gulab by long letters on the duty of continence and the importance to husband and wife of staying apart. Not surprisingly, she had a nervous breakdown.

Gandhi was the first to admit that he was full of human faults, but the ones most noticeable to others were the ones he could not combat because he did not perceive them. He was a man of piercing, but narrow vision, capable as we have seen of fighting racial intolerance in Africa without really considering the plight of the African native. In consequence, he tended to look at questions exclusively from his point of view. It was natural for him to dominate other people out of earnest desire for their ultimate good. But while he was careful to ask them to make up their own minds about his suggestions, he could never be satisfied while they disagreed. He once spent part of a voyage arguing with a friend about his extravagance in possessing a pair of binoculars. He never convinced the owner, but eventually his persistence gave the bone of contention so much importance that he was able to ask whether a mere possession ought to come between them. Wearily the friend agreed it should not, and Gandhi tossed the offending object overboard. Similarly, he was capable of saying to his opponents, "I would be most happy to be convinced if I am wrong," infuriatingly unconscious that what he really meant was: "I know perfectly well I am right, but if you could have convinced me that I was mistaken I should have been happy to admit it."

These characteristics of his father were hard on Harilal, who felt overwhelmed by a personality bigger than his own. But it was not merely in relation to his son that Gandhi showed them. Already he was yielding to a determination to dominate the Indian struggle down to the last detail. Meanwhile, in the heat of controversy, he was permitting himself to call General Smuts a murderer because the wife of one of his supporters suffered a miscarriage when her husband was arrested for breaking the law. Nor could he see that the position of moral superiority that he was anxious to maintain must suffer when he thus gave way to unreasonable anger. Like all great propagandists, he found it hard not to be carried away by his own words.

Though for the sake of the cause Gandhi did not court arrest, he was of course not carrying a registration card. This made it possible for the Transvaal government to pick him up as he returned from Durban in October 1908. Once more he asked for the maximum punishment and was given two months, this time at hard labor.

It was an unpleasant, at times a terrifying experience. He had always kept himself in shape by regular walking, but he was slight in build and in any case not accustomed to heavy road-gang work. He did not complain, though the guards shouted at him to work harder, taking pleasure in their power over the Indian leader. Presently, he was removed to Johannesburg to testify in some cases coming up, and here he was locked up with Chinese and Kaffirs, the scum of the Johannesburg jail, vicious types with whom he could not communicate in any language. Here he literally feared for his life, but was soon fortunate in being removed to a cell with other Indians.

He served his full two months this time, and before he reached the end received the news that Kasturbai was ill. He wrote to console and encourage her, but the cause he served was more important. For two weeks after his release he did not hurry to her in Phoenix. When he did so, the doctor told him that she needed surgery. It was performed in a private hospital in Durban, where Gandhi stayed a few days with her, only returning to Johannesburg when she seemed slightly better. A short while later the doctor telephoned to say that her condition was most grave and he had ordered strengthening beef tea.

Gandhi took the first available train to Durban in the conviction that Kasturbai, like himself, would rather die than eat meat. In this he was undoubtedly right, though she was too weak to make the decision or even to know that the forbidden food had been given before her husband arrived. Gandhi was furious, but the doctor insisted that without a free hand he would treat the patient no longer. Gandhi saw there was nothing to be done but to take Kasturbai away, though it seemed almost certain that the move would kill her. Somehow or other he got her to the station and helped her onto the train for Phoenix. Albert West was waiting for her there with a hammock, six bearers and a bottle of hot milk. Amazingly, she survived the trip, as well as the hemorrhages that followed, together with the hydropathic cures prescribed by her husband and his insistence that she give up salt and the pulse peas that were a favorite part of her vegetarian diet.

Gandhi returned to Johannesburg, was once more arrested for failure to carry a registration certificate, and was given another three months at hard labor. This time the government had decided on solitary confinement. For the first ten days, nine hours a day, hard labor consisted of polishing the asphalt floor of a cell ten feet by seven and its iron door. There was little ventilation and insufficient light to read by. There was no furniture in the cell, not so much as a bedboard or a mattress, and when he was later given blankets to sew together, he had to squat on the floor in a position that gave him a backache.

He did his best under these conditions, repeating poetry to himself, most especially that of an Indian friend called Rajchandra, whom he admired for his spiritual gifts. Standing up under the feeble light, he managed some reading, and solved the problem of one letter a month by sending an epistle of enormous length to Manilal at Phoenix, full of instructions about how everyone there ought to behave under every circumstance that he could imagine.

He was released in May 1909. By now the struggle had been going on for nearly two years. It had attracted attention not merely in India, but in newspapers around the world, for the novel tactics of *Satyagraha* had made some sensation. It had not, however, accomplished its aim, nor did it seem likely that it would ever do so. The Indian community, or at least that part of it supporting Gandhi, was too small to force the government's hand. Nor did moral victories, as had been hoped, convert the Europeans. In despair, Gandhi decided on a last appeal to London.

The Raggle Taggle Army

GANDHI'S TRIP to London in 1909 proved a waste of time and campaign money. His purpose had been to bring the influence of distinguished Englishmen to bear on General Smuts and his colleague General Botha, who were in England discussing the formation of the Union of South Africa. In the realistic world of politics, the fate of a few thousand Indians was not sufficiently important to hold up negotiations on a great issue. Smuts was easily able to put off Gandhi's friends with empty phrases. Meanwhile Gandhi himself, seething with frustration and nervous reaction from the strains of the past year, was turning against not precisely England, but the whole civilization she represented.

Though Gandhi was the first to use nonviolent protest as an organized political movement under modern conditions, he was not the inventor of the nonviolent idea, which is even older than Jesus and is embedded in Hindu as well as Christian tradition. Nor was Gandhi even the first in his own day to think along these lines. Nonviolence already had its prophet, whose name was Leo Tolstoy.

Gandhi's debt to Tolstoy was immense, and he read every-thing that he could lay his hands on by the extraordinary Russian. Basically they were much alike, though Tolstoy was more impulsive, far more unstable, less practical, a great creative artist who was not gifted with the talents of the politician. He shared with Gandhi enormous energy, pre-occupation with personal goodness, and a desire to impose his message on the world. Like Gandhi, he was a great patriot, intensely attached to a country that was autocrat-ically governed. His struggles with the Tsarist regime were always muted by the consciousness of its importance to him as characteristically Russian. Eventually, he solved his prob-lem by rising above it to condemn not Tsarism, but all the political systems of the world. Power is another name for force, which is the opposite of the great Christian principle of love. In other words, Christian governments, by becoming governments at all, have turned away from Christianity. The Christian life can only be lived in a small community where all is common and love of one's neighbor takes the place of lawcourts, police or military power. Such a gospel does not pretend to solve a great many questions. It merely appeals to the kind of man to whom Jesus once said, "Follow Me."

In 1909 and 1910, when Gandhi started a correspondence with him, Tolstoy was in his last year of life, a white-bearded sage of tremendous reputation to whom people wrote about their personal problems from everywhere in the world. He had never heard of the inventor of *Satyagraha* and recorded in his diary: "Received a pleasant letter from a Hindu in the Transvaal." Nevertheless, he answered kindly, giving Gandhi permission to translate his "Letter to a Hindu," in which he argued with a young Indian revolutionary. The correspond-ence continued, and a year or so later the last long letter of Tolstoy's life was written to Gandhi.

This correspondence with Tolstoy is interesting only because Gandhi was in a real sense Tolstoy's successor. It was far too fragmentary to have any influence on him, as apart from Tolstoy's other writings. This is a pity, for one of the troubles about Gandhi was that he seldom if ever met his equal in ability or outright moral worth. Tolstoy was his match, besides being just as domineering, and exactly twice his age. Gandhi needed such contacts.

The message of Tolstoy sank deeply into Gandhi's heart because it reinforced a growing conviction that Western civilization was all bad. He detested its false standards. During his visit to England, Louis Blériot flew the English channel from Calais to Dover for the first time. Gandhi's comment when he read the acclaim in the papers was that: "No one points out what good it will do mankind if planes fly in the air." Besides, Indian nationalism had taken extreme forms in London; and Gandhi had come in contact with a terrorist leader called Savarkar who was many years later to play a part in his own murder. Savarkar talked to all who would listen about the sufferings of India and the crimes of the English, many of which were genuine enough. Gandhi, incapable of hating the English, whose empire he still admired, transferred his dislike to the civilization whose impersonality and money-making greed had ruined India.

He worked this argument out in a famous pamphlet called *Hind Swaraj*, or *Indian Home Rule,* which he wrote in nine days on the homeward voyage, scribbling so fast he had to use his left hand to write when the other got tired. It took the form of a dialogue between an inquiring terrorist called "Reader" and an "Editor" who was Gandhi himself and always got the best of the discussion. Basically his theme was that the Indian village was the unit in which the good life could be lived. He drew an ideal picture of its rural elders, its hereditary occupations and traditional religion, pointing out that each knew his appointed place, lived by the work of his hands, served his neighbors and progressed in simple virtues. What benefits had Western civilization conferred? Were they to be found in the teeming slums of Calcutta or the vast system of railroads merely serving to spread disease from place to place or to provide transport for pilgrims who had far better walk? Modern medicine, he admitted, might save lives; but was it worthwhile to develop a science based on the cruelties of vivisection in order to preserve life for a soul that would in any case be born again? *Hind Swaraj* called on India to turn back to her traditional ways. The British would be welcome in India on a man-to-man basis, provided that they conformed to the customs of the country, abstaining, for instance, from eating beef to please the Hindus and from eating pork to please the Muslims. Meanwhile, let Indians turn back to India and find in their own traditions their national soul. In South Africa Gandhi had preached adaptation to Western ways, but he would do so no more.

This utter rejection of European values, this determination to turn the clock back is characteristic of Gandhi's political thinking from this time on. It deserves a little thought, for in the first place, the ideal village life that Gandhi accuses the British of having destroyed, never really existed in the period in question. Gandhi is looking back to the great traditional epics of the Hindu sacred books where gods and heroes fought on earth, as they fought with the Greeks and the Trojans. With a curious blindness that is characteristic sometimes of a great propagandist, Gandhi never admitted — even if he saw — this fact. Nor did he consider the economic problems that would arise from peacefully deserting the mills of Calcutta or the industrial

port of Bombay. Like Tolstoy, he rose above these questions, asking pertinently, "What values does Western civilization offer that we have not got in ourselves?" He answered,
"None." This attitude can make sense in a prophet, such as
Tolstoy, or a preacher. But Gandhi at every stage was also
a practical politician. It was this prophetic quality that confused the British, accused with passionate conviction of de-
stroying a civilization that had never been there; and it also
confused Gandhi's political heir, Jawaharlal Nehru, urged to
reduce India to her primitive self and never bother his
head about her governmental problems. Yet difficult though
this made Gandhi to deal with, it introduced a concern with
true Indian values into the struggle for independence. Furthermore, it infused the masses with a patriotic fervor that
could never have been aroused by exhortations to become a
great modern state.

His son Harilal found him hard to deal with also. Harilal's jail sentences had given him a good deal of time for
thought. By now he was thoroughly bitter about Gandhi's
treatment of himself and his young wife, about his refusal
to educate his sons, and about his domineering behavior to
their mother. Arguments between the two got nowhere, for
Gandhi always took a high moral view and could never come
down to Harilal's plane. The inevitable end was a break
between them. Harilal left for India to enter high school at
twenty-three amid boys of fifteen or sixteen. He wrote from
time to time, but it had to be recognized that he would go
his own way despite his father. Gandhi, who had given his
own father unlimited reverence, never understood Harilal's
attitude or reflected that old Karamchand had died before
he himself was a man. Thus the breach was never healed;
and the father, so patient with all other men, showed himself unforgiving.

The *Satyagraha* campaign was going badly when Gandhi returned from London. Only a limited number had been willing to go to jail for months or even years. Their sacrifice had inconvenienced the government and made some stir in the outer world, but it had not caused the slightest change in South African opinion. Campaign funds were running low, and all were discouraged.

The situation was saved by Gokhale, now a member of the Viceroy's Council and highly respected by everybody who mattered in India. Through his influence, money began to come in to Gandhi from such unlikely sources as Ratan Tata, greatest of Indian industrialists and representative of that westernized India that Gandhi had just been denouncing, or maharajahs whose selfish accumulation of wealth he openly deplored. It never mattered to Gandhi where money came from; the only question in his mind was how to use it. At the moment he needed a place where wives and children of his imprisoned followers in the Transvaal could be cheaply supported while their breadwinners were in jail.

He talked over plans with Hermann Kallenbach, an architect of German-Jewish descent with whom he had been intimate for several years. Kallenbach, who was well-to-do and had no dependents, bought and gave Gandhi a farm about twenty miles outside Johannesburg containing eleven hundred acres with a good-sized house and about a thousand fruit trees, which could provide an important part of vegetarian diets. Tolstoy Farm, as Gandhi at once decided to call it, was ideal for his purposes, capable of supporting a community housed in simple buildings and a convenient distance from Johannesburg. He himself could walk there and back in a single day!

Tolstoy Farm occupied Gandhi far more than Phoenix Farm because he could generally live there. In it he worked out those notions about an ideal community that had begun to dominate his thinking. He even rejoiced because his human material was extremely various and by no means all in love with community living. The wives and children of Gandhi's male supporters, who ended up at Tolstoy Farm while their husbands were in jail, had no more chosen this sort of life than Kasturbai. Not all of them were prepared to like it. Then too, a nature such as Gandhi's attracts a certain amount of the flotsam and jetsam of society. Gandhi would never turn away misfits, eccentrics, people who were psychotic or diseased. As he pointed out, a representative community must serve a proportion of such people.

He plunged into the organization of the farm with joy, taking on himself to decide everything from sanitation to morning and evening prayers and communal meals. But it was characteristic of him that he did not give orders. He was sure he did know best, but others had to agree that this was so; he would be satisfied with nothing less. He wanted not obedience, but consent. Similarly, though he acted as judge, priest, father confessor, sanitary inspector, treasurer, purchasing agent and schoolteacher, he did not consider that these duties exempted him from chores. He took his place with everyone else to help in the kitchen or to take his turn at cleaning up.

It is perhaps in the education of the children that Gandhi can be seen at his best and at his most outrageous. The job was peculiarly his, not only because of his interest in children, but also because at the start of Tolstoy Farm he and Kallenbach were the only really educated people in it. His first concern was to be worthy of the task, so that he redoubled his efforts at self-examination, lying awake for hours to ponder over all his problems. As a teacher, he was less concerned with academic studies than with spiritual train-

ing — which may have been just as well because the children
were of all ages and of Hindu, Muslim, Parsee and Christian backgrounds. They would have required instruction in
Hindi, Tamil, Gujarati, Sanskrit, Urdu and English, in only
three of which was Gandhi at all fluent. He soon abandoned
textbooks, except for asking the children to learn hymns and
devotional poems. Lessons became discussion groups with a
strong moral and religious emphasis, or simply stories.

Generally speaking he got on well with the children, despite differences in ages and upbringing. He could put himself on their level with complete absence of pretension. His
smile was as charming as ever, and the mischievous look of
little Mohan had never left him. He liked a gentle joke at
somebody's expense. His difficulties with the children chiefly
concerned the adolescents. On the one hand, he mixed boys
and girls together far more freely than Indian families usually permitted. On the other, he expected them to live as
unself-consciously as he now lived with Kasturbai. Naturally
he perceived that he must be vigilant, especially as children's
habits were often already formed before they came under
his care. He could not prevent some incidents. Once two
of the girls had attracted a certain amount of teasing from
the boys. After a sleepless night pondering the problem,
Gandhi decided that the girls would have to protect their
purity in some way that would be visible to all. He therefore
suggested to the girls as punishment that they submit to
having their heads shaved. They were not prepared to agree,
and some of the women — no doubt including their own
mothers — took their part. But Gandhi when aroused was
irresistible. His great prestige, his mildness of manner, his
endless arguments and his unwearying persistence won the
day. The girls gave in, and Gandhi had the last word. The
incident, as he was happy to point out, put an end to flirting.

Since this was his attitude toward the merest hint of trouble, it may well be imagined that his feelings overwhelmed him when something serious actually occurred. What had he left undone? How had he failed? What should he do to reform the sinner? Stealing, lying and other juvenile sins made him miserable. Probably he noticed that his own distress affected the culprit more than a punishment. After some years, in a really scandalous case of misbehavior, he was moved to announce that he himself would assume the burden of guilt; and as a penance he imposed on himself a fast of seven days, to be followed by one meal a day for four months and a half.

This self-imposed fast revealed to Gandhi a weapon he was to use time and again. As he did so, he learned the technique of managing fasts so that he was able to prolong them considerably beyond seven days. On this first occasion he suffered greatly, and the whole community, including those who were guilty, saw him do so. Gandhi's indomitable will subdued them with loving cruelty despite themselves.

The *Satyagraha* campaign, whose momentum had been slightly increased by the establishment of Tolstoy Farm, soon dwindled again to nothing. As long as the government refrained from arresting people who were not carrying cards, it was hard to keep up enthusiasm for breaking other laws. The situation had drifted into a stalemate. Gandhi was forced to turn to other methods; and in October 1912, he persuaded Gokhale to come to South Africa in person.

As a minister of state and personal friend of the Indian Viceroy, Lord Hardinge, Gokhale could not be ignored by the South African government. An official railroad car was placed at his disposal for a month-long tour, engineered by Gandhi, which took in Indian communities throughout the Union. Unfortunately, Gokhale had diabetes and was at this time in failing health, so that it was only by an extraordinary effort that he managed to complete his exhausting schedule. This in itself accentuated friction between two men who liked and admired each other but were both used to having their own way. Hitherto Gokhale had been the great man and Gandhi the learner. Now they were equals and on Gandhi's ground.

He lost no time in advising Gokhale to cure diabetes by giving up tea and coffee, eliminating cooked food gradually, and taking brisk country walks. He should also fast frequently, restrict himself to two meals a day, and abstain from condiments of any kind. Gokhale laughed at him and called him a quack, but Gandhi persisted, as always.

Next they had a dispute about Gokhale's speeches. His only Indian language was Marathi, which was little spoken in South Africa. Sooner than have him speak in English, Gandhi was prepared to translate him into Hindustani. Gokhale objected, knowing that Gandhi's Marathi was very limited and his Hindustani no better than fairly good. Gandhi argued until Gokhale gave in, murmuring resignedly, "You will always have your way." It was a phrase that Kasturbai had also employed to her husband.

They went out to Tolstoy Farm by train from Johannesburg to the nearest station whence, instead of arranging for transport, Gandhi persuaded the invalid to try a nice brisk walk. Unfortunately, it rained. Gokhale caught a cold and found that conditions on the farm were very primitive and no arrangements had been made for his comfort. Gandhi tried to remedy matters by fussing. Gokhale must have his feet massaged and submit to other attentions, which increased his misery. He snapped at Gandhi, who received reproof with pained astonishment.

The truth was that though Gokhale submitted to Gandhi's

arrangements, he did not like them. He hated public receptions, presentations, banquets, noise. It embarrassed him to listen endlessly to his own praises. His real purpose was to discuss the Indian problem with Botha and Smuts, for quiet diplomacy was his preferred method. He was elaborately briefed for the meeting by Gandhi, who saw on the one hand that Gokhale would get further without him, but imagined on the other that nothing could be done properly by anyone but himself. Actually Gokhale made an excellent impression and was able to assure Gandhi that the Black Act and the three-pound tax would both be abolished. Gandhi said he doubted this and turned out to be right in principle if not in detail. "Asiatic Affairs" were transferred from the provincial governments to the federal one. The Black Act vanished because it applied only to the Transvaal, but it was replaced by restrictions that were nearly as bad and applied to the whole Union of South Africa.

Thus Gokhale came and went with little effect on the Indian position in South Africa. Gandhi had played his strongest card in vain, and it looked as though he were a failure. In March 1913, the situation took a sudden turn for the worse as the Supreme Court of Cape Colony handed down a decision invalidating all marriages not celebrated by Christian rites. Indian wives became concubines and their children illegitimate. It was actually dubious whether the women had a right to remain in South Africa, even if their husbands were on the voting lists.

There was no appeal against the Court. Meanwhile, Gandhi's army of *Satyagrahis* had by this time dwindled, according to his own account to sixteen people, plus fifty more to whom he could appeal. A fair number of these last were women, including Kasturbai, to whom he had explained the meaning of the Supreme Court judgment. He had decided that it was time for her to take active part in the work.

Gandhi's faithful followers were concentrated in Phoenix and Tolstoy Farms, the first in Natal and the second in the Transvaal. Accordingly, the easiest way to court arrest was to travel between them — for none of his people owned registration cards, and in any case special permits were required for Indians moving from one province to another. Sixteen people from Phoenix Farm, including Kasturbai, started the new campaign by traveling into the Transvaal. On crossing the border they were arrested and sentenced to three months' hard labor. So far, so good.

Eleven women now set off from Tolstoy Farm to cross into Natal. As the Natal police left them alone, they went on to Newcastle, a mining town not far from the border. Here the coal mines were worked by indentured Indians among whom the women held meetings, persuading them to come out on strike.

This was going too far for the authorities. The mineowners retaliated by floggings, while the women were thrown into jail and sentenced to three months at hard labor. The miners, however, persisted; whereupon the owners cut off light and water supplies to the company shantytown. About five hundred miners deserted their shacks to camp on the farm of an Indian Christian who promised to feed them for a few days.

Rushing down from Johannesburg in great excitement, Gandhi found himself in command of a little army of nonviolent resisters. Their numbers increased daily, and friendly merchants from Newcastle were ready to provide them with food and cooking pots. Gandhi saw the mineowners, offering to call off the strike if the three-pound tax was repealed, but this came to nothing. He then decided that the entire body should march across the border of the Transvaal and court arrest. This would really fill the jails! It would also throw on the government the burden of supporting the strikers. He did not know how many they were, but thought they might be five or six thousand. Actually there were about two thousand, and each had a pound and a half of bread and an ounce of sugar a day to take them to the Transvaal border.

They started on November 6. Gandhi explained that they were to take no personal belongings, were to respect the property of anyone on the way, and must bear patiently whatever the Europeans inflicted on them. Under these orders they straggled up to Charlestown on the border, sleeping at night by the wayside. The police arrested one hundred fifty persons and proposed to take them back to Newcastle, but since they had no conveyances ready and Charlestown was nearer, they marched them on with the rest and were forced to buy them provisions.

Charlestown had about a thousand inhabitants, including a few Indian merchants who opened their houses and gardens, providing food that was cooked in the local mosque. A few more miners joined the marchers with the news that the Newcastle owners were relying on strong-arm methods to keep the strike from spreading any further.

There were rumors that some of the Europeans of the Transvaal were ready to shoot down anyone who crossed the border. Gandhi was worried and decided on a last-minute appeal to General Smuts. He telephoned Pretoria, telling Smuts's secretary that if the general would promise to abolish the three-pound tax, he would call the march off and take the miners back to Newcastle. The secretary spoke to the general and came back to the telephone with a message: "General Smuts will have nothing to do with you. You may do just as you please."

On the following day at 6:30 in the morning, Gandhi set

off with his army for the border after holding prayers and giving his instructions. There was a gate across the main road between Charlestown and the Transvaal border town of Volksrust. Here on the Transvaal side mounted police were waiting.

It was a moment at which anything could have happened. The miners, though obedient to Gandhi as though to a saint or holy man, were not really disciplined. It was important from Gandhi's point of view to avoid a riot, for the citizens of Volksrust were reported to be arming against the invasion. Walking up to the police at the gate, he engaged them in conversation, while a signal was given to the army to rush, not at the gate, but across the open country on either side of it. This they did; and the police, caught by surprise and far outnumbered, were thrown into such confusion that they did not even arrest Gandhi, who lined his people up and marched them on past Volksrust in the general direction of Tolstoy Farm, still eight days off.

They camped in a field that night; but just as Gandhi was about to go to sleep, a policeman with a lantern came çautiously past his sleeping followers to tell him that he was under arrest. He was allowed to leave instructions that the men start marching before sunrise and that they be given the news of his arrest when they halted for breakfast. Arrangements had been made by Kallenbach and Sonja Schlesin; other workers from Tolstoy Farm had joined the marchers. Women with babies were from now on to travel to Tolstoy Farm by train. Among the miners, there had been 127 women and 57 children at the beginning of the march.

All was very well in hand, but Gandhi improved the occasion by a forceful telegram to the Secretary of the Interior, disclaiming all responsibility for what might happen if he were not allowed to continue with the men. It was even possible, he said, embroidering freely, that women with children in their arms might perish if the miners were left leaderless; and in that case responsibility for their deaths would lie with the government.

These arguments prevailed, at least with the magistrate before whom Gandhi was brought in Volksrust, who immediately released him on fifty pounds' bail. He rejoined the marchers and a day or so later was re-arrested and released in the same fashion. But by this time the government had made up its mind what to do. Gandhi was arrested for the third time, taken to Volksrust, and sentenced to nine months' imprisonment with hard labor. He was sent to serve his sentence in the Orange Free State which, under strict immigration laws, had no Indian community.

Meanwhile, the government solved the problem of the miners by rounding them up, sentencing them to imprisonment, designating the Newcastle mines as their prison, and enrolling the company foremen as special constables to act as guards. This ingenious solution failed of its purpose because no kind of ill-treatment could compel the prisoners to mine coal. They might be poor, ignorant men, but they had marched in an army under a leader of genius who had shared with them an ideal.

Gandhi's imprisonment lasted little more than a month. The Union of South Africa had not reckoned with Gokhale's influence in India. Suddenly the struggle of South African Indians against their government had become an international affair. Lord Willingdon, Governor of Bombay, said publicly that it was a question in which the whole British Empire must be concerned. The Viceroy of India spoke of the sufferings of the Newcastle miners with "deep and burning sympathy," adding that passive resistance had been dealt with by "measures which could not for one moment be tolerated by any country that calls itself civilized."

Naturally the Union of South Africa was highly incensed, and Smuts and Botha pressed for the Viceroy's recall. But India occupied a peculiar position in the British Empire. Though not self-governing, she was immensely the largest single portion, the training ground and great recruiting center of the British army. In fact, in a very real sense the British Empire in the East *was* India, while the Union of South Africa was small in population and had been conquered by imperial arms only ten years before. These facts could not be overlooked by the British Cabinet, which was not prepared to recall its viceroy. It fell back on a commission of inquiry. To be sure, the commission contained no Indians and had three members of a strongly anti-Indian bias. But the Viceroy sent an envoy to South Africa to represent the Indian view to the commission, while Gokhale sent two British missionaries, one of whom, Charles Andrews, was an influential and remarkable person.

Everyone always liked Charlie Andrews, who was a man with remarkable understanding of alien cultures. He was a friend of India's great Hindu poet, Rabindranath Tagore, and intimately connected with a foundation for the arts that Tagore had established. He had never met Gandhi, but their attachment was immediate and lasting. Indeed, many years later when the Mahatma had long ceased to be greeted as an ordinary man, it was observed that Charlie Andrews was the only person in the world who called him Mohan.

Andrews was important because he knew everyone and was as skillful in negotiation as Gokhale. On this occasion, he was well acquainted with Lord Gladstone, Governor-General of South Africa. Thus during the preliminaries of the discussion that was to follow, he was quietly meeting with important members of the South African government. South Africa was paralyzed by a railroad strike, and Gandhi, now released from jail, was asked whether the Indians would join the strikers. Gandhi saw no reason for this, since the grievances of the railroad men and those of the Indians had nothing in common. It was Andrews, however, who pointed out to him that much might be made of his generosity in refusing to embarrass the government at an awkward moment. When the matter was put this way, not even Smuts himself could fail to be grateful.

Negotiations were eventually opened between Smuts and Gandhi after the ground had been well prepared. General Smuts, who had started out by despising Gandhi, was coming to feel reluctant admiration for his peculiar opponent. Difficulties that had seemed insuperable began to disappear. It was agreed the three-pound tax should be abolished, Indian marriages should be recognized, the Black Act should be done away with, and the entry of educated Indians into Cape Colony should be permitted.

This was victory at last after eight years of struggle. Gandhi was suffering from nervous reaction, and Kasturbai after her prison experiences was seriously ill. Gandhi's work in South Africa was finally over. He thought of returning to India, but for some reason decided to go to England first. He sailed in July 1914, loaded down with farewell addresses and leaving behind him a present for General Smuts, a pair of sandals he had made in jail. The general accepted them in the spirit in which they were given and wore them around his farm for many years. In 1939, he returned them to Gandhi on his seventieth birthday as a keepsake. By that time both were men of world importance, and Smuts was able to say that there had been no hatred or personal ill will throughout their struggle. In a sense this is true; but the general's most candid opinion of Gandhi in 1914 was best expressed in a letter to a friend remarking, "The saint has left our shores, I hope for ever."

He had indeed left forever after a victory whose nature might have given him food for thought. *Satyagraha*, the force of truth, had won the battle, but not the war. Gandhi's methods had welded the Indians together; they had brought about changes in the law; but they had never affected the racial views of white South Africans. The repealed laws were in time replaced by others, and South African Indians today are a "colored" race in a country where only white men count. Their fate is a commentary on *Satyagraha*, which achieved a limited end without ever changing, as Gandhi thought it would, the atmosphere.   ·

The Man from Champaran

THE INDIA to which Gandhi returned in January 1915 was
a country to which he had only paid scattered visits since he
was eighteen years old. It was a country of five hundred
million people, some two thirds of whom were ruled directly
by the British and the rest by a crazy patchwork of Indian
princes. Its great towns, swollen into appalling slums by
factory labor, were the ports of Bombay in the west, Calcutta
in the east, and Madras in the south. The ancient centers of
the country, which lay inland, were in many cases much as
they had been for centuries, only more crowded and dirtier
and with the addition of a British quarter. The vast bulk of
the population still lived in villages of which there were about
seven hundred thousand.

The achievements of the British had been patchy. They
had established internal peace and the rule of law; they had
put down the worst of the professional robber gangs and
were constantly waging war on what remained. They had
covered the country with a network of railways and had

developed an efficient technique for dealing with the famines common among people dependent on the arrival of the rains. In northwest India they had developed the largest system of irrigation works known to man, settling millions of people on virgin soil that had been desert. They had fought a creditable battle against plague, cholera, and other epidemic diseases, though these still took a serious yearly toll.

The chief failure of the British, which was at least as important as their achievements, was to make any considerable impact on local custom. It was not that they admired Hindu-Muslim culture. On the contrary, their rule would have been more creative if they had understood it better. But it was their deliberate policy not to interfere with the traditions of the country, except in flagrant cases like the Hindu practice of burning a widow alive with her husband's corpse. The wisdom of this decision had been confirmed by the one bloody episode in Anglo-Indian relations, the great Indian Mutiny of 1858, which had been triggered by suspicion of British reforming zeal. Undoubtedly British tolerance made their autocratic rule possible; yet as the rule grew older, a thoughtful eye could perceive the necessity of changes that needed the consent of the Indians themselves.

For an example, we may take the birthrate. To a Hindu, it is the family that matters; and this can only be carried on by sons. Early marriage gives a man extra years in which to be fruitful. Harilal Gandhi, who was actually his father's second child, was born when his parents were eighteen. Despite frequent long absences from his wife, Gandhi had begotten five children by the time he was thirty. Internal peace, irrigation, war on famine or on disease merely swelled the Indian population and made poverty more abject and decent sanitation, education, or other experiments more hopeless. Yet when the British ventured to introduce a law

against the marriage of very young children, Tilak, the fiery advocate of Indian independence, fought against it tooth and nail. It was not that Tilak, a highly educated man, did not perceive the evils of child marriage; but he resented any interference with Indian customs, holding that Hinduism must be reformed from within.

A failure of a different sort was the existence of over six hundred princes, some ruling over estates as large as France and others over country towns like Porbandar. These potentates were people with whose ancestors the British had made treaties, generally in the course of the eighteenth century. At the time, these agreements had saved trouble and left large parts of the country under Indian rulers. As a result, the rajahs, ranis, and thakores were confirmed in their possessions, apparently for ever. Occasionally the British had replaced impossible rulers, and they had been careful about the education of princely children; but no change had ever occurred in the relation of the prince to his subjects. He remained their absolute sovereign who, even in the changing times of the twentieth century, did what he pleased.

Nationalism, which as we have seen was given focus by the biennial meetings of the Indian National Congress, was confined to educated people, that is, to the towns. Educated Indians were as a group underemployed and underpaid. Owing to the reluctance of Indians to labor with their hands, this being an occupation reserved for the lower castes, there was little demand for technical education. Everybody wanted to study liberal arts, in English; and most often the available teachers did not know their subject really well. In consequence, men with college training were often fit for little; and few opportunities were open to them. As underlings in the civil service they performed a task vital to the British administration, but far from satisfying to an able

Gandhi and his wife Kasturbai on their return to India from South Africa in 1915 man. Thus besides outstanding leaders like Tilak, Gokhale, or Gandhi, who had made a success of journalism, law, or education, there was an ever-increasing group of discontented people.

The British for their part had given thought to Indian nationalist demands a few years earlier. Perceiving that nationalism was not deeply rooted, they had been cautious, questioning the ability of a country still ninety percent illiterate to govern itself. However, they had enlarged the legislative councils of the provinces, included elected or appointed Indian members as well as officials, and had admitted Indians, among them Gokhale, to the Viceroy's Executive Council. More importantly, they had announced these reforms as a start on the way to self-government.

To all this Gandhi was essentially a newcomer. To be sure he was in his forty-sixth year and had achieved remarkable things in South Africa; but he was out of touch with Indian realities. Gokhale advised him not to make public utterances, but to observe and travel for a year. Gandhi saw the wisdom of this, but he was in the position of a successful general who has suddenly been reduced to a junior lieutenant. He had not reached middle age and some celebrity without forming both his character and opinions. What was more, the times required urgent decisions. Two days before Gandhi had landed in London, England had entered the First World War. After agonized thinking about where his duty lay, Gandhi had once more offered to head an ambulance corps. After all, he was demanding not independence but home rule for India. In the pages of *Hind Swaraj,* home rule is in practice equivalent to independence; but then so was the home rule of Australia, for instance, or even of the newly formed Union of South Africa. What Gandhi envisaged was a friendly agreement between India and England, a partnership on equal terms. This is a position that cannot be extorted by rebellion, but must grow out of mutual understanding. Gandhi was as sure as ever that Indian support in a crisis would win the gratitude of England. Naturally he could not have made this decision had he not also been outraged by German militarism and convinced that England was supporting the right cause.

He enlisted his men from Indians in London and duly went into training with them. His health, however, had by no means recovered from the strains imposed on him by the South African campaign. He collapsed with pleurisy and tried to treat himself by giving up cereals and milk and living exclusively on nuts, bananas, lemons, tomatoes, and olive oil, besides keeping his windows open night and day, despite the rain. Persuaded at last that he could not live through the English winter, he left for India and in 1915 was facing the problems of where to live and what to do with his life.

This time he had no intention of practicing law. Gone forever were the starched collars and sober suits. In South Africa he had taken to wearing the long white Indian coat with a *dhoti*, in the form of a wraparound skirt reaching to his ankles. The wealthy supporters whom he had gained through the help of Gokhale had given him the chance to devote his whole time to public affairs. It is true that both his brothers were now dead and, as head of the family, he had responsibility for women and children; but Tolstoy Farm had convinced him that a large group of dependents could live in simplicity at minimum cost. For his own part, the community life was all he wanted for the future.

He decided to live near Ahmedabad, which was Gujarati-speaking and situated at the landward end of Kathiawar. It was thus in home territory, while at the same time it was nearer the center of things than Rajkot. Ahmedabad was a textile town, an industrialized part of the new India. Big capitalists there were prominent among Gandhi's supporters. With their aid, a community arose on the banks of the Sabarmati River in full view of the smokestacks of Ahmedabad.

Community life at Sabarmati was modeled on that of Tolstoy Farm, except that Gandhi made greater demands on the inhabitants. Permanent members had to take nine vows; to tell the truth, refrain from violence, live celibate lives, control the pleasures of eating and drinking, refrain from stealing, possess nothing, wear no foreign cloth, fear nothing, and accept untouchables. Sabarmati lived, in other words, under monastic discipline, mingling vows of asceticism and moral behavior with others devised by Gandhi to combat special Indian problems.

From the beginning he was determined to admit untouchables, those unfortunates numbering nearly ten million who were not allowed to use the public wells or public highways, who must live apart, feed on carrion and other refuse, and occupy themselves as scavengers. Gandhi was delighted when an untouchable with a wife and daughter applied to the community, but Kasturbai was roused to make a protest about this outrage against her whole traditional set of values. She threatened to leave, and he stormed at her; but he had his own way as usual. The untouchables came, and Gandhi was so delighted by the little girl that he adopted her as his own, always speaking of her as such. More serious than the revolt of Kasturbai was the disapproval of the wealthy merchants of Ahmedabad. Money ceased to come in; and Gandhi was desperate enough to think of moving to the untouchable quarter of Ahmedabad, which would have been cheaper. However, just when things were at their worst, an automobile drove up to Sabarmati and its owner, a wealthy man whom Gandhi did not know, put an envelope into his hands and drove away. Inside it were thirteen thousand rupees. The crisis was averted.

Sabarmati was home to Gandhi, but he always traveled extensively. There were meetings of Congress to attend, trips to famous temples or holy spots for the purpose of seeing India. He was outraged by Indian dirtiness, disgusted by the avaricious priests, the squalor of the temples, the professional beggars, the lying and the stealing among the Indian poor as they fought one another for a living. But his reaction to disorder was to pitch in and clear it up whenever a chance arose.

He did not see much of India's rulers, for he was out of sympathy with the civil servant in his neat bungalow enjoying English living standards and a modest pension, or with the maharajah, living in splendor on the vast revenues he drew from his subjects. But once, just a year after he came to India, he found occasion to say what he thought of them all.

Conspicuous among Indian leaders at this time was Mrs. Annie Besant, the only English person ever to preside over the Indian National Congress. Annie Besant, a tireless and gifted worker for radical causes, had been converted to Theosophy at about the time that Gandhi was studying in England. Taking over the movement when its founder died, she had transferred her headquarters to India. Here she had come into contact with Indian nationalism and had adopted it with vigor, putting at its disposal not merely the force of a remarkable personality with long experience of public work, but the resources and auxiliaries of the Theosophist movement.

Among Mrs. Besant's achievements in India had been the

foundation of the Central Hindu College at Benares in 1892. Twenty-four years later it had prospered under her guidance to the point of being transformed in a public ceremony to the Hindu University of Benares. It was a memorable achievement which was honored by splendid ceremonies. The Viceroy himself formally opened the new university in the presence of maharajahs, important English dignitaries, and educators from all over India. Mrs. Besant could have her choice of men to speak on the occasion; and many speeches were planned, among them one from Gandhi.

It is difficult to know why Mrs. Besant picked out Gandhi, whose South African victories were a little out of date and whose reputation in India could not compare with those of other people who would have to be crowded off the program. Possibly with the acumen that was characteristic of her, she had already marked him as a coming man, or perhaps she put him on the program as a saint. India has its own idea of holiness, differing in various ways from the Christian ideal, since a holy man is generally one who renounces the world for the sake of his own soul, rather than one who does good or leads men to God. Gandhi, however, had accompanied his renunciation of wealth and pleasure by dedication to a life of service. This made him interesting to a westerner like Mrs. Besant, while at the same time his unworldly qualities appealed to the masses. The very sight of a holy man is thought to convey a blessing to a Hindu, so that wherever Gandhi went there was already a commotion aroused as much by his holy reputation as by his record of Indian nationalism. In other words, he possessed a distinction that was not run-of-the-mill; and Mrs. Besant might have found it hard to get this peculiar blessing from any other source.

Everybody appeared in his best costume: the Viceroy with his medals, the military with theirs, the civil service people correct in heavy formal suits, the maharajahs studded with jewels, and Mrs. Besant, in herself a formidable presence, dressed from head to foot in white. Gandhi in a coarse white cloak and clumsy *dhoti* looked out of place and may have felt so. At all events, his speech was delivered in a loud, almost angry voice very different from his usual gentle tone; and it penetrated to the farthest corners of the hall.

He started out by attacking the speeches for being in English, which was generally used on public occasions as the only language common to educated Indians. Having thus criticized the learned world for being too English, he went on to criticize the Indian scene, in particular the holy city of Benares for the indescribable filth of its Golden Temple. This led him on to the dirt of the third-class railroad carriages, owing partly to the general habit of spitting in them. Then, turning to the Indian potentates, he upbraided them for sitting resplendent in their silk and jewels while such conditions existed. Was not their wealth raised from the poor?

The dignitaries sat stunned, but Gandhi's daring had caught the imagination of the students. Leaving the Indian princes to simmer with rage, he turned on the Viceroy, whose presence in Benares had been preceded by an army of police, rummaging into every place from which a bomb might have been tossed. What a pity! Gandhi went on to praise not precisely the bomb throwers, but their daring, their love of country. He hoped that he himself, if he ever decided that the British should quit India, would die for that belief, even if not precisely by throwing bombs. Skillfully repeating the idea, he hammered home his admiration for the patriots who dared such deeds.

This was almost incitement to violence. Mrs. Besant burst out, "Please stop it!" Some of the princes started to leave

Gandhi, wearing white hat, in 1922 while campaigning to ban liquor in India

the dais. Students shouted to Gandhi to go on, while others yelled to him to leave the platform. The Maharajah of Darbhanga, who was the chairman of the meeting, got up and walked out, so that speech and meeting broke up in confusion.

Gandhi had made a sensation, angered privilege, and outraged Mrs. Besant. A few of the students, however, had been delighted at his plain speaking. Among them was Vinoba Bhave, who soon became a member of the community at Sabarmati and a favorite disciple. Too independent to be content as a satellite of Gandhi, he founded a community of his own and, after partaking in all of Gandhi's campaigns against the British, became at last his spiritual heir. He represented in free India the thoughts and ideals of the saintly Gandhi, whose more political side was developed by Nehru.

This episode at Benares gave Gandhi a reputation for being a dangerous radical, but it did not offer him a place in Indian life. His real career was started by someone much more unlikely than Mrs. Besant, an obscure little Indian peasant called Rajkumar Shukla who turned up at the Indian National Congress in December 1916.

Rajkumar Shukla was a man desperately in earnest who

wanted to talk in his broad dialect about the sufferings of
tenants on indigo plantations in Bihar. He came from a district called Champaran in Bihar, which nobody seemed to
have heard of, with a story that was too confused to understand. He took his troubles to Tilak, who replied that his
time was entirely occupied by political agitation and he had
none left for local grievances. Even the delegates from the
province of Bihar made little of Rajkumar Shukla. Peasants'
problems were hopeless to disentangle. They kept no records, lied freely and did not know how to present a coherent
case. Besides, the nationalist movement did not depend
on these dumb millions but on the townsmen, who could
understand national issues.

Failing elsewhere, Rajkumar Shukla came to Gandhi, who
could hardly comprehend his rough dialect. When he perceived this, Shukla brought in a lawyer who was one of the
delegates from Bihar. Gandhi did not like the man, who was
suspiciously prosperous and might, he suspected, be in
league with the oppressors of the indigo workers. The conversation trailed off as Gandhi told the pair of them to bring
their problem before Congress. He himself could give no
opinion without seeing conditions with his own eyes.

Without troubling to understand the subject, Congress
passed a resolution calling for redress. Meanwhile, Rajkumar Shukla made up his mind to get Gandhi to Champaran.
He pressed the point persistently, but Gandhi said he had an
engagement in Cawnpore. When he got there, who should
be waiting to see him but Rajkumar Shukla. "Champaran is
very close to here," he insisted.

Once more Gandhi replied that he did not have time. He
went back to Sabarmati, but Rajkumar Shukla followed him,
begging for just one day in Champaran. Gandhi suggested
the following March when he was going to Calcutta; but

when he got there, Rajkumar Shukla was not present. As he left again, Gandhi received an agitated message. There had been a misunderstanding about dates, but would he please keep his promise and come to Champaran? He replied that he would be in Calcutta again in another month, and duly arrived to find Rajkumar Shukla waiting.

The two went off by train to Patna, which was the largest city near the district in question and a place where Rajkumar Shukla said there was a movement of protest. But when they arrived, they found none. Local lawyers, whom Gandhi had expected to find busy with the peasants' grievances, knew nothing about them. Rajendra Prasad, the particular lawyer whom Shukla said he knew, was out of town. Shukla had suggested that Gandhi should stay in Prasad's house and did succeed in persuading the servants to let him spend the night; but they denied him the use of the common well and latrine, not knowing his caste.

By this time, Gandhi had lost all faith in Rajkumar Shukla and was little wiser, because he could not speak the local dialect. He did remember, however, that a distinguished Muslim leader whom he had met in London was living in Patna. He went to him for advice and was told that there was indeed an area in the province where the peasants were in revolt against factory owners. He was put on a train for a place called Muzaffarpur, while his Muslim friend telegraphed to an acquaintance that he would arrive there at midnight.

Gandhi got out at Muzaffarpur barefoot and wearing a coarse *dhoti*, carrying nothing but a little box of refreshments, which was indispensable to an Indian train journey. Immediately he found himself the center of a crowd shouting, "Gandhi! Gandhi!" Enthusiastic people took the horses out of a carriage and dragged him through the streets to the place where he was lodging.

The following morning a group of lawyers and teachers assembled to explain the matter to him. The owners of indigo factories in Bihar had long ago enslaved their peasants, working them for a minimum wage and demanding that three twentieths of their holdings be planted to indigo, which was to be delivered to the factories as rent. As early as 1860, the misery of the district had attracted the attention of the Governor of Bengal, who had attempted to enforce reforms. But the indigo magnates had a powerful lobby, and the Governor had been recalled to England. Since that time, they had done what they pleased.

In the early years of the twentieth century, synthetic dyes began to take the place of indigo, leaving the factory owners with a worthless product on their hands. Accordingly, they offered to release the peasants from the three-twentieths in return for handsome monetary payments. Not until after a great deal had been paid did the peasants discover that the indigo for which they were paying was worthless. They attempted to resist their masters, who imprisoned or killed the leading agitators and forced the rest to go on paying. Meanwhile, the price of indigo went up again as a result of World War I; and the indigo merchants began to insist once more that large areas be planted. In addition to all these demands, there were special levies that the owners had grown used to exacting at their pleasure.

Assimilating these facts, Gandhi laid down the outlines of a new strategy. Legal proceedings to recover some of what had been paid were hopeless. They cost more than peasants could afford and dragged on forever, merely fattening the purses of the lawyers. What was needed was a painstaking accumulation of facts acquired by a band of investigators who must give their time free and be prepared to suffer if the authorities attempted to disperse them.

The lawyers listened with astonishment. Rajendra Prasad, who soon caught up with Gandhi and consented to be head of his committee, replied that the middle classes of Bihar were not remarkable for their devotion to acts of public service. Nevertheless, the idea caught on. As Nehru said long afterward, it was difficult to exaggerate the impact of Gandhi in those times. Intelligent people could not escape the miseries of India. They were all around them, but on so vast a scale that nobody had any idea where to begin to tackle them. As townsfolk, educated people were divorced from the life of the countryside, which was the real life of India. Thus leaders talked about grievances, and Congress passed resolutions, but nothing got done. Gandhi took these frustrated men and plunged them into action. His demands on them were high, but he offered a chance to come to grips with problems that had been vexing their consciences for many years. In consequence, contact with him was fruitful; and to no one was it more fruitful than to Rajendra Prasad, who was to devote his life to public service and to become the first president of free India.

Gandhi opened his campaign by announcing to the district authorities his intention of going to Champaran to start an inquiry. Responsible for law and order and regarding Gandhi as an agitator, they ordered him to leave the district. Taking his stand on the resolution passed by Congress, Gandhi retorted that he had been authorized by Congress to look into the facts, which was to one vowed to literal truth at least stretching a point. It did him no good. The reputation of Congress in official eyes was lower than Gandhi's. It began to look as though he would be arrested.

Perceiving the danger, he set out at once, arriving by train at Motihari with two interpreters in attendance and changing there onto the back of an elephant. He landed in a village called Chandrahia, which was quite empty because everyone was working in the local indigo factory. Here he was caught by a policeman on a bicycle, who escorted him back to Motihari, where an order of expulsion signed by the district magistrate, a Mr. Heycock, was waiting.

Gandhi refused to leave and communicated his intentions not only to Mr. Heycock, but to various Indian leaders, the private secretary of the Viceroy, and Charlie Andrews, whose presence might, he felt, calm authorities down. By the time he was brought to court on the following day, he had made a start on taking depositions and arranged for the inquiry to go on if he were imprisoned.

His trial took place before Mr. Heycock and was attended by about two thousand peasants, who tried in vain to jam their way into the courtroom. Perceiving that Gandhi's imprisonment would arouse the very riots he was trying to avoid, Mr. Heycock postponed sentence for three days while he consulted the Lieutenant Governor of Bihar. Gandhi, prevented from going out into the villages, found that the peasants came streaming in to him, so that the inquiry went on as briskly as ever.

Sir Edward Gait, the Lieutenant Governor, besides hearing from Mr. Heycock, heard in no uncertain terms from Gandhi's friends, who represented that an inquiry into facts was not agitation. He ordered that the case be dismissed.

But the case had served its purpose by drawing attention to Gandhi throughout the district. When he finally set out by train through Champaran with the proud Rajkumar Shukla, crowds of peasants were waiting at every village halt to receive the blessing conferred by a vision of the saint.

At Bettiah, where he got out, the crush on the platform was such that the train had to be stopped a little distance away for fear of accidents. Once more his carriage was dragged through the streets; he was pelted with flowers and followed by joyful crowds crying, "Gandhi! Gandhi!" Rajkumar Shukla basked in his day of glory, but very shortly disappeared into the obscurity from which he came.

The inquiry was soon in full swing with Gandhi surrounded by secretaries and interpreters who were in private life important men and who had come, as it were, on safari, bringing cooks and bearers to do the manual work that was beneath them. Anyone, however, who wanted to work with Gandhi had to live as he did. Worn out by his persistence, inspired by his capacity to get things done, and conquered by his charm, men let their servants go, became vegetarians for the duration, rose for prayers an hour before dawn, and trotted after their new master, panting to keep up with his walking pace.

In a few weeks' time Gandhi had accumulated some four thousand depositions, and the evidence against the planters was damning. Even worse than their financial exactions had been their reign of outright terrorism, which had prevented the peasants from daring to seek redress. They now were using harrassment against Gandhi, but the flow of people eager to tell their story was so great that no reprisals could stop it. Naturally, the local newspapers were in the magnates' hands and influence was brought to bear on Sir Edward Gait. It was taken for granted by the indigo men that the government would be on their side.

In this assumption they were wrong. Sir Edward Gait was a fair-minded man with the best of intentions, who was well aware that the situation in the Champaran district was a scandalous one. Like everyone else he had lacked evidence.

It was now clear that he was going to get this, and he was disposed to take it seriously. Accordingly, he summoned Gandhi for a series of meetings in which he proposed a commission of inquiry with Gandhi as one of the members. He even consented to let him act as judge and prosecutor too, presenting the evidence he had gathered from the peasants, which eventually reached twenty-five thousand depositions.

Not surprisingly, Gandhi proved his case to the commission, which awarded the peasants a twenty-five percent return of illegal exactions. This result is characteristic of Gandhi. By forcing any restitution at all he had destroyed the planters' prestige and the source of their power. This being the case, he thought it better to work out a compromise than to insist on full payment.

The affair of Champaran made an extraordinary sensation. A new day had dawned for India, and those who took part in the inquiry had seen it. For the first time, a man had gone to the villages and had tackled the troubles of India in the place of their real origin. He had shown that the masses could be aroused and that the government would bend to their pressure. He had taken middle-class people and turned them right around, made them live with villagers in village style and do practical things more important than all their discussions. Above all, he had descended on villagers and townsmen alike almost in the guise of a visitor from heaven, if only because he was so odd that his like was not seen on earth. Who else got up at four in the morning for prayers? Who else lived on nuts and fruit and had taken a vow not to eat more than five different foods in a day? Who else was so untiring, so demanding, so charming and so personally unselfish?

Battle Between Brothers

The Champaran affair established Gandhi as a potent force in Indian life, and to him personally it was a first intimate contact with the masses. He was appalled by the miseries of Champaran and attempted to improve things by founding simple schools in selected villages, importing members of the Sabarmati community as teachers. He even included Kasturbai in the number, despite her illiteracy and the fact that she knew no Indian language but Gujarati. The children, he pointed out, needed training in cleanliness, not grammar. Even he was shocked when Kasturbai at his direction asked one of the women why she never washed her clothes. In answer, she led Kasturbai into her hut, so bare of furnishings that there was no pot in which to do washing. The sari, she explained, was her only garment, so that she could not take it off and wash it in public.

Except in the case of Gandhi's successful defiance of the magistrate's order, he had found little chance for a display of *Satyagraha*. Nevertheless, the experience as a whole reinforced his conviction that *Satyagraha* would be more effective than force. A test of its usefulness on a larger scale was soon offered him in Ahmedabad, at the very gate of Sabarmati.

The mill workers of Ahmedabad were typical of a first generation of industrial workers who are drawn from a rural area where the pressure of poverty is extreme. In other words, they were ill housed, ill paid and bewildered. There had recently been an outbreak of plague in the town, which had stimulated the mill owners to pay a bonus of seventy percent to those brave enough to stay on their jobs. The epidemic passed, and it was proposed to cancel the arrangement. Prices, however, had soared during World War I, and the workers claimed that they needed a cost-of-living bonus. They asked for fifty percent, but the owners would only agree to twenty percent. On his return from Champaran, the workers appealed to Gandhi, who recommended a compromise of thirty-five percent. This being rejected, Gandhi found himself once more in command of an army prepared to strike under his leadership. He took immediate charge, so impressing himself on the workers that they behaved peaceably, encouraged by daily meetings with Gandhi beneath a tree on the bank of the Sabarmati.

Conspicuous among the owners was Ambalal Sarabhai, the very man, it is always supposed, whose thirteen thousand rupees had saved the community at Sabarmati. At all events, he was an especial admirer of Gandhi through the influence of his sister Anasuya, who was widely known in Ahmedabad for her charitable works. The close affection between this brother and sister was not damaged by the fact that Anasuya took the workers' side, visiting among them and using her resources to fend off starvation or find odd jobs of work. As a result, the struggle was conducted in peculiar terms.

Among the workers, Gandhi would not permit abuse of the mill owners, always speaking of them as well-intentioned men with mistaken views. In similar fashion, the owners did not resort to violent methods.

For about four weeks the workers held firm until starvation stared them in the face. At this point the owners offered twenty percent, which was rejected by Gandhi as insufficient either for the need or in the light of textile profits. But by the fifteenth of March only a few people gathered to hear Gandhi under the tree by the banks of the river. Even these were heard to mutter to one another: "After all, Gandhi Saheb and Anasuya-behn have nothing to lose. They move about in cars, and they are well fed."

The reproach was only too true, and Gandhi felt it. The strikers had their lives at stake while he did not. In fact, he could not steel their wills any longer without descending to their level. "Unbidden," he records, "and all by themselves the words came to my lips: 'Unless the strikers rally and continue the strike until a settlement is reached, or until they leave the mills altogether, I will not take any food.'"

Men crowded around him completely overcome and offering to fast instead of him until victory was reached. He had to dissuade them, telling them that it was enough if they held out. He found occupation for some in shifting sand from the river bank for the foundations of a new weaving school in his community, thus paying, one may presume, with funds from the mill owners for continuation of the strike.

Workers rallied to Gandhi, but his conscience troubled him. His gesture, though made on impulse and purely for the sake of the workers, had put the mill owners in an impossible position. Unless the strike were settled, he would die. There were several others besides Ambalal Sarabhai who were personal friends and had contributed to the community at Sabarmati. Thus it was not merely that Gandhi had saddled his opponents with the potential guilt of his death; he had done it to his friends.

With this in mind, he readily advised the workers to settle for thirty-five percent, which now proved acceptable to the owners, horrified by his novel form of blackmail. The strike ended in happy agreement, only marred by a scene when the owners offered ceremonial sweetmeats to the workers under Gandhi's famous tree. So many beggars came out in Ahmedabad to infiltrate the ranks of the genuine workers that what had been intended as an orderly distribution ended in a stampede. Gandhi was left to ponder the effects of *Satyagraha* and of the fast that he had used for the first time as a public weapon. He could not quite exempt himself from blame for blackmailing the owners; but as a practical man he saw the gesture had worked.

On the whole, this episode went against the grain with Gandhi. In his usual practical way he continued to interest himself in the welfare of the mill hands, supervising a union that he encouraged in many community activities. Labor troubles, however, had meant a struggle of Indian workers against Indian employers. He had pitted Anasuya against her brother Ambalal. Gandhi did not like his position, and with relief he turned back to rural problems.

While all this was going on in Ahmedabad, in the district just outside it the peasants of Kheda were in an uproar about paying their taxes. It was the custom in times of scarcity for the government to remit taxes if crops were less than a quarter of the normal. Unfortunately decisions on these matters depended on the local district officer, a British official to whom all peasants lied on all occasions. Thus in the Kheda case he had made the wrong decision, so that the peasants were taxed beyond their ability to pay. In despair,

they took their case to an Ahmedabad lawyer named Vallabhbhai Patel, a successful man who, as one might suppose,
could not be expected to have much time for charitable work.

In appearance, Patel was a stocky man who looked as
though he had been carved out of something hard. His
voice was deep and brusque, his manner determined, and his
expression aggressive or roughly genial. A man of humble
background, he had risen to success in Ahmedabad through
an ability that was actually so great that he was still unsatis-

Gandhi with Vallabhbhai Patel, who was to become a major force in
the construction of a new India

fied. Lonely after the death of his wife, he needed something into which to pour his pent-up energies. Of farming stock himself, he understood the predicament of Kheda. Undertaking the case, he appealed for help to Gandhi, now famous for his work at Champaran. Together they organized a tax-paying strike. Patel, discarding his Western clothes and reverting without effort to the manner in which he had been brought up, toured everywhere, eating and sleeping among peasants, inexhaustible, never forgetting a face, and using his rough, jolly manner to remarkable effect. Gandhi marked him down as a future leader and proved to have discovered a political organizer of genius who was to have a major hand in the construction of the India to come.

Meanwhile, the peasants of Kheda, after four months of nonviolence, won a compromise, by which the government exempted the poorer peasants on whom taxes pressed hardest. This was no victory, for either all taxes should have been remitted or none, since the harvest had been the same for everyone. Gandhi felt dissatisfied, but a government bent on collecting taxes is a tough enemy, especially in the last year of a world war.

Things were going badly for the allies as victory over Russia gave Germany a last chance to break through in the West. Men were needed for a final stand, and the Viceroy held a conference of Indian leaders in Delhi, hoping they would stimulate the flow of volunteers. Gandhi responded with his last great effort for the British Empire, which he still idealized as a stabilizing influence and thought capable of generosity toward its subject peoples. Once more he wanted India to deserve the gratitude that victory, as he felt sure, would bring. In consequence, he made a tour of Kheda, where a short while earlier he had been assisted with bullock carts to get about, offered free lodging, and welcomed as a saint. Then he had been preaching resistance to an unjust government. Now he was asking men to fight and die for their rulers. Indian peasants, however, were simple men to whom a government was either unjust or not, but never both. Gandhi, who had supposed himself a leader in Kheda, found himself traveling on foot and left to sleep out in the fields. It was instructive commentary on the limits of leadership.

The episode was also an interesting sidelight on Gandhi's own attitude· toward violence. He never pretended to be a consistent man, being too practical not to know that circumstances alter cases. Besides, he was not ashamed of changing his opinions. What is more, when we talk of Gandhi's operations in terms of "campaigns" or "armies" we express a truth. Gandhi was a natural fighter, and he knew nonviolence came close to violence — none better. He was prepared to use force in extreme cases, as for instance against a madman attacking a friend. By conceding this much, he laid himself open to argument. Does not extreme wickedness amount to madness? Is there not madness in the mass hysteria of war? May one country therefore resist attack by another? Gandhi never found occasion to apply violence himself, but he seldom utterly condemned it in others, content to dwell on nonviolent suffering as a higher way.

It was this nonviolent suffering that Gandhi was pondering as he tried to lay down principles for political action. The man who uses the nonviolent weapon, the *Satyagrahi*, must first make up his mind that he is right in thinking a situation to be evil. To be sure that this is so, he should confine himself to a simple demand like abatement of taxes or the righting of a particular wrong, never letting himself get bogged down in generalities, which tend to shade off into points of view. Having fixed on his demand, he will get his way by suffering in protest until the heart of his opponent is melted. He may do this by breaking simple laws and going to prison, by disobeying orders, by striking peacefully, and even in some cases by a fast. While he acts, he will never cease reasoning with his opponents, seeking to appeal to minds as well as hearts. Even death will not matter to the *Satyagrahi*, because his cause will go on. *Satyagraha*, as Gandhi conceived of it, is a group movement.

Many problems arise in applying *Satyagraha* to political action. Who is to know that a *Satyagrahi* is in the right? The answer is, only he himself. Suppose, then, he is mistaken. He must be open to conviction by his opponents. May everyone decide he is right whenever he sees fit? Will this not bring utter confusion? Gandhi never answers such questions because it seems to him that truth is simple and open to the earnest inquirer. *Satyagrahis* who truly seek enlightenment will all be of the same mind. What, however, of the followers who may be inflamed by a grievance but do not understand the principle of *Satyagraha*? In an illiterate land like India there must have been many such. Gandhi was prepared to use these men as instruments, realizing the risk he was taking in stirring up passions, but preparing to restrain them as far as he could. He was even willing to use men who did not believe in nonviolence, merely finding it a useful technique for getting their way. Gandhi was a practical man. Yet though he might lead such forces and could not always control them, he generally counted himself a failure when violence broke out. Near the end, it is true, he preferred to blame the British for having removed him from control of what he had unleashed.

Amritsar

E<small>NGLISH</small> <small>GRATITUDE</small> for Indian services in the First World War took the form of the Government of India Act of 1919, which marked a new stage in British-Indian relations. Though the constitution of 1909 had implied that the aim of India should be self-government, it was left for the Act of 1919 to define the form of government intended for India as a parliamentary one, and to set up institutions that might give Indians practice in ruling themselves. The provincial councils were now made into parliaments with a majority of elected members restricted, however, by a narrow franchise. They were given control of education, agriculture, health, and other internal matters, subject to official control over finance and law and order. At the central level a bicameral legislature was created, again, with the majority elected. The Indian Civil Service and the police force, hitherto dominated entirely by the British, were to be increasingly Indianized. It is true that the Viceroy, still advised by a council containing both British and Indian members, had power to override this constitution, but in actual fact he very seldom did so. Most important of all, the Government of India Act was to be reviewed in ten years.

This constitution, which established a division of rule between British and Indians, defining the areas of each, was disappointing to Gandhi and the nationalists, who had hoped to get more. Nevertheless, the concessions were considerable and might be expected to produce more liberal changes in ten years. It seemed to be in the interest of India to cooperate, so that all might have gone smoothly, had India been a country at peace within itself, economically prosperous, and detached, as it had hitherto been, from the rest of the world. India after a world war was no such country.

The trouble began with the British, whose defeats in World War I had seriously damaged their prestige in India. No longer invincible in Indian eyes, they faced a revolt in Ireland, which gave the Indian extremists fresh inspiration. Meanwhile the Russian revolutionaries, whose terror tactics had always found some Indian admirers, had overthrown the Tsars. Peace, followed by the return and demobilization of troops, was also bound to have unsettling results. Seditious activities, which had died down in the excitements of 1914, had by 1918 revived so alarmingly that a commission headed by Mr. Justice Rowlatt had been appointed to investigate the problem. The Rowlatt report, embodied in a bill of 1919, recommended such severities as secret trials for suspected terrorists and imprisonment for possession of seditious documents, followed by a parole period during which activities of the culprit should be drastically restricted.

The difficulties of the government were no doubt real, but one thing was certain: England could not offer a liberalized government with one hand and the Rowlatt Act with the other. By this time, Gokhale was dead, and Tilak died suddenly in 1919. Thus Gandhi, whose reputation was swelling like an oncoming tide, was soon the national leader who could command the greatest following throughout the country.

Since the Rowlatt Act embodied precisely the sort of highhanded behavior that Gandhi could least tolerate, his rejection of it was immediate. Actually he was still weak from an illness that had followed on the frustration of his recruitment campaign in Kheda. He had in part brought this on himself by giving up almost all kinds of food but ground nuts and lemon, and making a vow to abstain from milk forever in protest against Hindu mistreatment of milch cows. If there seems something almost absurd about Gandhi's food habits, it must be remembered that his concern was not merely with self-discipline. He actually did not want to eat more than a minimum as long as so many of his countrymen went underfed. On this occasion, his life was only saved because Kasturbai suggested that goat's milk might be considered outside his vow. Gandhi gave in, but with a bad conscience. He had not in fact thought of goat's milk one way or the other, but he felt it ought to have been included in the vow. For the rest of his life he was always looking without success for some way to cut goat's milk out of his diet.

At the time of the Rowlatt Act, he was still weak, but he managed to travel across India, though his voice was too frail to reach a crowd and most of his speeches had to be read for him by Mahadev Desai, another lawyer from Ahmedabad, who had given up his profession to become Gandhi's secretary. Gandhi wanted to start some form of *Satyagraha* in protest against the bill, but thought it ought not to be a personal act. It should be a national demonstration. He brooded over the fearsome problem of arousing a nation of inarticulate millions to do he knew not what. Between waking and sleeping one day, the idea came. A *hartal!*

A *hartal* is an Indian day of mourning when all shops close and business stops and people go to the temples or pray. No one had ever thought of a *hartal* on a national scale, but the plan suited Gandhi exactly. In the first place a *hartal* was peaceful. In the second, it was well within everybody's competence, requiring no breaking of laws or sacrifice beyond the one day's wages. It did not require enthusiasm to be kept up among those who were not ready to take part in a sustained national effort. All it needed was that India should be quiet for a day and that the silence should be felt by her rulers.

The idea of the *hartal* was a stroke of genius. In the villages, perhaps, it would not be kept, but in these places there was no bustle anyway. In every town, great or small, there would be a nationalist group headed by some local man with friends or following. There were even the underemployed and the unemployed, the ragged people who would shout with a crowd for the fun of doing something or threaten to loot the shops that did not close. A *hartal* organized across the length and breadth of the land was not going to be all quietness. On the contrary, it turned out to be a thing of mass processions, placards, speeches, fiery threats. In that first moment of glorious inspiration, Gandhi had not reckoned with its getting out of hand. But though he gave his followers careful instructions, many of the leaders had little contact with him personally and had their own methods of operation. In Madras, for instance, the Indian public was told that the Rowlatt Act included physical inspection of couples before marriage and prohibited even family parties of over two or three people. It was never likely that a crowd aroused by such methods would be perfectly controlled. That splendid hush that Gandhi had foreseen was to be broken not only by the roll of oratory, but also by the occasional yell of a crowd gone mad.

Gandhi himself led the *hartal* in Bombay, which was a city where he had briefly lived and was well known. Under his influence, vast crowds assembled on the beach to purify themselves by wading into the sea. Everything in the great city came to a standstill; and that evening Gandhi himself in a slow-moving automobile, accompanied by Sarojini Naidu, a well-known Indian poetess and one of his prominent disciples, sold copies of *Hind Swaraj* and his Gujarati translation of Ruskin's *Unto This Last*, both banned by a government that was at least intelligent enough to disregard the provocation.

In Delhi, the Indian capital, things went less smoothly. In a remarkable demonstration of solidarity, a venerable Hindu leader had been invited to speak in a Muslim mosque. Impressive in the yellow robes of a holy man, he led a huge procession up the main street of Old Delhi, where Gurkha troops tried to break it up. There was firing, and nine people were killed. Feeling ran so high that the Delhi leaders appealed to Gandhi to come in person. But the prospect of his arrival was too much for the British, who pulled him off the train at a little station and told him that he was under arrest. After wondering for a few hours what to do, they took him back to Bombay and released him. He was greeted by crowds gone wild with joy, for the news of his arrest had spread already. Gandhi started to speak, but mounted police armed with iron-tipped staffs charged the crowd and broke it up. He hurried to the police commissioner to complain, but that official had no time for pledges of nonviolence. He had no doubt, he said, about Gandhi's intentions; but the people misunderstood them. He would do his duty by dispersing crowds. Gandhi protested that the people were by nature peaceful.

The commissioner knew better. Reports of riot were coming in over the telegraph. At Ahmedabad, the crowd had burned the office of the commissioner of police. Telephone wires had been cut, railroad lines ripped up, and Europeans murdered. The mill hands, lately so devoted to the principles of *Satyagraha,* were rioting in the streets.

Gandhi was aghast. He traveled to Ahmedabad and by the magic of his presence restored order, but he sadly admitted that he had been mistaken about the people. More tragic news was to follow, for Gandhi did not yet know what had happened to Amritsar.

Amritsar was a holy city of the Punjab in the northwest part of India. It was Sikh country, where men were accustomed to carrying swords. There were the usual parades until the authorities became alarmed as news of violence at upcountry railroad stations or severing of telegraph lines seemed likely to cut Amritsar off from the rest of the province. Under the orders of Sir Michael O'Dwyer, governor of the Punjab, the civil authorities tricked the two chief Amritsar leaders into a conference, at which they were summarily arrested and deported. Presently a mob of threatening appearance came rolling out of the narrow streets of the old city toward the British quarter with the intention of rescuing their men. There was general panic among the British. Women and children were hastily collected, and messages were sent into the town to fetch in everyone to a place of safety. The available troops were native ones, few in number and not steady. Their commander lost his head and ordered them to fire. The crowd scattered and rushed back to the old town, where they took their revenge by wrecking two British banks and hacking to pieces their unfortunate clerks, as well as a couple of railroad employees who had not received the message to abandon their posts. Miss Sherwood, headmistress of a missionary school who was doing some innocent errand, was attacked and left for dead. Amritsar was utterly out of control, while the terrified British community thought that another Indian Mutiny was on them. Frantically they wired for reinforcements.

These arrived under the command of General Dyer, an Indian army man who had made his reputation in the brutal little frontier wars, where an expedition that neither got nor granted any quarter was sent to teach marauding tribes a lesson. By the time Dyer arrived, Amritsar was quiet, for the bulk of the citizens were horrified by what had happened. He established martial law and sent out criers with drums to announce that public meetings would be prohibited until further notice. He did not put up posters, reasoning that most of the inhabitants could not read them.

In the confusion, nobody saw to it that the announcements were made all over the city. Indeed, presumably because they were afraid to penetrate too deeply, the police in charge had made the proclamations in open spots where few assembled to hear them. In consequence, the prohibition was not generally known, especially since rumors of all sorts were humming about. There was, moreover, a Sikh festival a couple of days later, which attracted many visitors from the country. All in all, it was not surprising that a meeting was arranged in a large wasteland in the center of the city which, inappropriately, was called Jallianwalla Garden. About six thousand people gathered there in orderly fashion, around a speaker on a central platform.

General Dyer, who had been informed in the course of the morning that the meeting was due to take place, made no move to stop it. On the contrary, he waited until everybody was gathered before rushing to Jallianwalla in an armored car, accompanied by fifty troops armed with rifles and forty more with heavy native swords. Abandoning the car because it would not penetrate the narrow street leading to the garden, he came into it on rising ground, which gave him a view of the central hollow already filled with the people around the platform. Deploying his men to cover the other exits, Dyer ordered them to fire into the crowd until their ammunition was exhausted.

They did so as the frantic people fled shrieking. Many attempted to get out over a five-foot wall that was close to the soldiers, making the fugitives excellent targets. Altogether about fifteen hundred people were shot, and three hundred and seventy-nine of these lay dead. With them in a very literal sense died the British Empire. General Dyer marched his soldiers off, congratulating them on having done their duty and forbidding the citizens of Amritsar to venture out of their houses to succor the wounded.

In the ensuing days, General Dyer seemed to go a little crazy in his determination to teach "those natives" a salutary lesson. On the spot where Miss Sherwood had fallen, he erected a whipping post, decreeing that every Indian who passed by should do so on hands and knees or face a flogging. Other ordinances followed. High-school students were forced to salute the flag night and morning and, owing to the school schedule, some had to walk as many as sixteen miles in order to do so. Schoolboys were flogged, five hundred students and professors were arrested, hostages were taken. Utilities were cut off to Indians. Automobiles were confiscated so that General Dyer's forces could parade the town.

This horrible episode revealed even more about British weakness than that a general with lifetime service in India could treat the populace in such a fashion. There had to be an inquiry, and two Indians were chosen to sit on it. But the British members, in a majority, had not the courage to condemn Dyer outright. Many people in Amritsar, and indeed across the breadth of India, spoke of General Dyer as the man who had single-handedly averted another Mutiny with its massacres of whites, its Black Holes of Calcutta, its dry wells full of human bodies, and its improvised prisons ankle-deep in the blood of women and children. General Dyer was retired — he had to be — but he was not dismissed and kept his pension. His supporters in England presented him with a sword of honor and thirty thousand pounds, a very handsome fortune. British people had lost their nerve, and the low value they had for those they ruled was dreadfully apparent.

Swaraj in a Year

IF THE ROWLATT ACT first turned Gandhi against the government, the massacre at Amritsar gave his opposition a personal
edge, which in such a man was the equivalent of hatred. His
pride was revolted by the outrage of the infamous "crawling
order" which, being applied as it happened to the mouth of
a dead-end street, struck at harmless residents in a way that
was worse in his eyes than loss of life. Nothing would have
satisfied him but the disgrace of Dyer, accompanied by that
of the Governor, Sir Michael O'Dwyer, whose responsibility
was brought out in the inquiry. Thus though he had called
Satyagraha off in a hurry, admitting a "Himalayan blunder,"
he was soon casting all the blame he could upon the British.
The disorders in Ahmedabad had been due to his own arrest
on the way to Delhi. Riots elsewhere had been provoked by
British handling of peaceful processions. In other words, he
closed his eyes to the fact that it is usually irrelevant who
makes the mistake in a confrontation between authority and
a mob. It is the situation that ensures that mistakes get made
and people are hurt.

Nevertheless, though Gandhi spoke of British errors, it was evident to him that he had not solved the problem of conducting a nonviolent campaign on a national scale. It occurred to him that he might continue alone, forcing his own arrest by breaking the regulation of the government that for the present confined him to Bombay. He notified authorities that he intended to do so.

The British were horrified. They, too, realized that riot at Ahmedabad and pandemonium in Bombay had been touched off by their ill-considered arrest of Gandhi for leaving Bombay. They could well imagine what would result if they seized him again. In forcible terms the authorities informed him that they would have to put down disorders with firmness and that the blood that was bound to flow would be on his head. In despair, he canceled his plan and for some months devoted himself to the peaceful purpose of promoting homemade cloth.

The community at Sabarmati had planted its fields to cotton, for this was textile country. Very shortly after its founding Gandhi began to ponder the feasibility of hand spinning and weaving. But though weaving still existed, thanks to being the monopoly of a special caste group, hand-spinning had died out around Ahmedabad. It was several years before someone discovered a wheel in a local lumber room and taught Gandhi how to use it. After experiments at Sabarmati, the wheel was improved, made more portable and simpler. By now, Gandhi had made up his mind that the decay of cottage industry was a more important cause of Indian poverty than the increase of the birthrate. Dependent on alternate seasons of drought and rain, the Indian farmer has little to do for several months a year. Spinning, even if ill-paid, was a supplement to his income that he could not afford to miss. Gandhi liked to draw pleasing word pictures

Gandhi at a mass spinning demonstration with Jawaharlal Nehru at the right

of rural India in the days before the British had flooded the country with manufactured cloth, describing the peasant sitting happily spinning, with his wife and children around him, spinning also.

Always a man of action, Gandhi personally undertook a regular task· of spinning every day and carried it out for the rest of his life in every situation. He himself wore nothing but homespun, or *khadi,* and asked his followers to do the like, thus giving them a uniform that became almost as effective as the black or brown shirts that were adopted in Europe during the twenties and thirties. Spinning and boycott of foreign cloth were, he proclaimed, not merely the duty of every patriot high and low, but the method through which India would work out her salvation and turn away from the corruption of the industrial West. So passionate was his conviction on this point that he even finally attempted to force members of Congress to pay part of their dues in homespun yarn.

Near the end of 1919, the ban on his traveling was lifted, and he began to crisscross India, still spreading his gospel of *khadi,* though his progress was anything but quiet, owing to the enthusiasm of the Indian masses for the sight of their saint. In *Young India,* the newspaper he founded to spread his message, he tried in the following year to reason with his admirers in a passage that deserves quotation:

> I have been ashamed to witness at railway stations thoughtless though unwitting destruction of passengers' luggage by demonstrators who, in their adoration of their heroes, have ignored everything else and everybody else. They have made, much to the discomfort of their heroes, unmusical and harsh noises. They have trampled upon one another. All have shouted at the same time in the holy name of order and peace . . . It is a task often dangerous, always uncomfortable, for the heroes to be escorted through a broken train of volunteers from the platform to the coach intended for them. Often it is a process which, although it should occupy no more than five minutes, has occupied one hour . . . The coach is taken possession of by anybody who dares, volunteers being the greatest sinners. The heroes and other lawful occupants have to reason with the intruders that they may not mount the footboards in that summary fashion. The hood of the coach is roughly handled by the processionists. It is not often that I have seen hoods of motors left undamaged by the crowds. On the route, instead of lining the streets they follow the coach . . . To finish the picture there is the meeting, an ever-growing source of anxiety. You face nothing but disorder, din, pressing, yelling and shouting there.

It is a memorable description of what Gandhi faced for many years.

During the later months of 1919, while Gandhi was pondering how to harness the enthusiasm of such crowds, anti-British agitation arose from a new and unexpected source. The British Empire in India had been the successor to the empire of the Moguls, Moslem invaders from the northwest who had conquered India and had also converted a large number of Indians to their religion. The Indian poor and especially the outcastes had been attracted by a faith that did not recognize their disabilities. In consequence, there were many millions of Muslims in India, concentrated perhaps in the northwest, but scattered to some extent throughout the land. Indistinguishable from other Indians by race, they included princely rulers and masses of peasants who, being drawn originally from India's lowest classes, had remained ignorant and poor.

On the whole, their British rulers tended to like the Indian Muslims, who were often warlike men and provided volunteers for the British army. Lacking an educated middle class, they were to a large extent outside the nationalist movement. Congress, though it had Muslim members, was largely Hindu.

The spiritual head of the Muslim world and in theory its ruler was the Caliph, the successor of the Prophet, who was and had been for centuries the Sultan of Turkey. When Turkey took the German side in the First World War, the rulers of India hastened to assure their Muslim subjects that they did not desire to seize the Caliph's possessions. War, however, has a habit of changing situations. The Arab world, long oppressed by Turkish misgovernment, was ready for revolt. One of the most romantic chapters of the First World War is the guerrilla campaign organized by Colonel Lawrence against the Turkish power in Arabia. By the end of the war, promises of freedom had been made to the Arabs which Lawrence of Arabia, stalking the corridors of Versailles in Arab costume, was determined to see incorporated in the peace treaty. None of the victorious powers felt sympathy with Turkey, which had in any case by now deposed the Sultan.

To the great embarrassment of the British, Indian Muslims who neither knew nor cared about the wishes of the Arabs were excited to frenzy by the suggestion that the holy cities, Mecca and Medina, should no longer be in possession of the Caliph. There was nothing that the British could do to satisfy this outcry. Nor were British statesmen disposed to favor Turkey, which had destroyed the flower of English youth at the Dardanelles. The Turkish Empire was bound to be dismembered, while the Turks themselves cared so little about the Caliph that a few years later they abolished the office.

The agitation about the Caliphate, called Khilafat in India, was directed by a couple of Muslim newspapermen called the Ali brothers. Presently Gandhi, naturally drawn to fellow Indians with a grievance, attended a conference with the Muslim leaders at which an agreement was reached. The gist of it was that Gandhi should support the Khilafat agitation, while the Muslims should consent to use nonviolent methods. They preferred, as they frankly pointed out, a fight; but since they were powerless against the British, they would consent to use the nonviolent weapon.

This alliance between the genuine grievances of Gandhi and the unrealistic Khilafat cause, between he who believed in nonviolence and those who did not, between the saint and a couple of second-rate agitators was at once so strange and so momentous that biographers often break down in describing Gandhi's motives. Giving up all attempt to understand them and arguing simply from results, they call it a crude political alliance entered into out of opportunism. This is absurd, for Gandhi was not that sort of man. It makes better sense to dwell on the consideration that weighed most heavily with him.

To Gandhi, Hindu-Muslim unity was fundamental. He cared about it far more deeply than other Hindu members of Congress. In *Hind Swaraj* he had advised the British to avoid beef because of the Hindus and pork because of the Muslims, simply because he felt that in a dispute between brothers, each must respect the scruples of the other. Thus in the Khilafat campaign whenever he was not parroting the Alis, he would admit that he cared little about the rights of the case. In his eyes it was a religious cause on which the Muslims had to decide and which he must support. This attitude, though understandable, does not exempt Gandhi from the charge that he was too ignorant of matters outside India to pronounce upon them. Nor could he rightly object to a British change of policy toward the Turks and Arabs, since he felt free to change his own mind when facts demanded it.

This Hindu-Muslim alliance made by Gandhi raised the possibility of a movement truly nationwide and supported by all the leaders of India's major groups. Gandhi's imagination was excited to plan a revolutionary campaign of great audacity. In sum, his idea was that the government of India would collapse if its subjects simply refused to cooperate with it. The difficulty was to organize such a movement. He designed it in four steps.

First, all honors, medals, and titles conferred by the British were to be surrendered. This purely ceremonial gesture would be used to serve notice to government and people that everybody who mattered was behind the movement. The second stage was far more drastic. All lawyers should give up their practices. All government officials should resign their jobs. All students should quit government-aided schools. As the lawcourts ground to a standstill, arbitration committees might be set up among the people. As education came to a halt, national schools might arise, not purely academic and in any case quite temporary. Gandhi was to campaign for Indian Home Rule under the slogan of "*Swaraj* within the Year." Thus, though he outlined substitutes for law and education, his real idea was to call upon lawyers, students, teachers, or civil servants for a year of political work.

Unquestionably he hoped that these measures would force the government to give full satisfaction to the Khilafat, Amritsar, and Rowlatt grievances and to grant the country virtual independence. Nevertheless, he was prepared with two more stages. The third step was to call on soldiers to lay down their arms and citizens to cease to volunteer. Finally, he planned a massive refusal to pay taxes.

On August 1, 1920, Gandhi sent an ultimatum to the Viceroy announcing his intentions, which were put before Congress at a special meeting held in September at Calcutta. There were many Congress members who still held to the methods of Gokhale; they wanted to make the new constitution work and extort further concessions from the British before the end of the ten-year period. Gandhi, however, with his enormous following, his concrete plan, and his Hindu-Muslim alliance, was irresistible. His effect on the politicians was as overwhelming as on the lawyers in Champaran. Negotiations had proved frustratingly slow; his action was a relief; contact with the masses was seen to be a necessity. Men were swept away even if they did not share Gandhi's conception of a free and ruralized India, reverting to her primitive life despite the West. Similarly, disciples of Tilak, though they believed in violent action, perceived that a mass movement along nonviolent lines had a better chance of success. Gandhi's dictatorship over Congress, which was to transform that organization from a middle-class conference to a national political party, dates from the Khilafat alliance and the September meeting.

It was necessary to reorganize Congress, for Gandhi by himself could not direct so vast a movement. A working committee of fifteen, which already existed, was given extra powers and packed with men dominated by Gandhi. Beneath it came an All-India Committee, and beneath that provincial committees with roots in districts, towns, or even villages. An ambitious program was undertaken to enroll permanent members to the number of ten million; and though this was not achieved, Congress soon possessed an organization with branches everywhere and local political workers responsive to instructions from above. A great fund-raising drive for a Tilak Memorial Fund of ten million rupees was also started. Much of the detailed organizing work was done by Patel, the Ahmedabad lawyer whom Gandhi had discovered when he was campaigning for the peasants of Kheda.

All these activities, which were launched immediately, went on at the same time as the national movement to bring the lawcourts and education to a standstill. Gandhi himself, pouring out daily articles in *Young India,* called for a "fight to a finish," describing the British Empire as "based upon organized exploitation of physically weaker races of the earth and upon a continuous exhibition of brute force." Meanwhile, he continued to tour the countryside in company with Muslim leaders amid scenes that tried his fortitude to the utmost.

> We had been taking meetings at Salem during the day, motoring to Bangalore, a distance of 125 miles from Salem, taking there a meeting in drenching rain

and thereafter we had to entrain. We needed a night's rest, but there was none to be had. At almost every station of importance, large crowds had gathered to greet us. About midnight we reached Jolarpet junction. The train had to stop there nearly forty minutes or stopped that night all those terrible minutes. Maulana Shaukat Ali requested the crowd to disperse. But the more he argued, the more they shouted . . . evidently thinking the Maulana could not mean what he said. They had come from twenty miles' distance, they were waiting there for hours, they must have their satisfaction. The Maulana gave up the struggle. He pretended to sleep. The adorers thereupon mounted the foot-board to have a look at the Maulana. As the light in our compartment was put out, they brought in lanterns. At last I thought I would try. I rose, went to the door. It was a signal for a great shout of joy. The noise tore me to pieces. I was so tired. All my appeals proved fruitless in the end. They would stop for awhile to renew the noise again. I shut the windows, but the crowd was not to be baffled. They tried to open the windows from outside. They must see us both. And so the tussle went on till my son took it up . . . He produced some effect and there was a little less noise. Peeping, however, went on till the last minute.

This article in *Young India* bears witness to the breathless pace at which it was written. Gandhi's thought flowed out headlong, and he still wrote with his left hand when he got tired. On occasion he dictated to Mahadev Desai and others, all for the sake of speed. And in the middle of the campaign, the daily spinning went on.

The spinning and the use of homespun were part of the symbolism Gandhi used to bring his movement down to the level of simple men. All could watch a bonfire of foreign cloth and see rich people bringing fine saris to put in the flames. All could see the flag of the new India, which Gandhi designed himself; red for the Hindus, green for the Muslims, and white for purity, with a homely spinning wheel placed in the middle. These things were more telling than his words, which frequently in the excitement of his meetings were not heard. But the most effective piece of symbolism resulted from his rage at the disorder of his meetings, and indeed at the total disorder of Indian life. Deciding to perform a penance on himself, he stripped to the loincloth which, with a pair of sandals and a shawl in case of cold, were to be from this time on his only garments. Thus he brought himself down to the dress of the poorest peasant when he is working his fields. It was a uniform that set Gandhi apart from every other Indian leader and daily emphasized his link with the poor.

The campaign for *Swaraj* in a year had the same effect on simple people that proclamations of the Second Coming have had in other places. There was a real fanaticism expressed by the students who had quit school, the peasants or shopkeepers who had settled their legal problems out of court. "Only for a year!" Short of actual starvation, much can be endured for a year. The picketing and intimidation with which these patriots tried to force their views on other people was distressing to Rabindranath Tagore, the Indian poet who had received the Nobel Prize and was universally respected in India. It was Tagore, incidentally, who had first saluted Gandhi by the title that had by now swallowed up his given name. He was the *Mahatma*, or the "Great Soul." Indians love such complimentary titles.

Tagore at least dared to express his opinion, and in a letter to *Young India* he complained of the oppressive atmosphere. "When I wanted to inquire, to discuss, my well-wishers clapped their hands over my lips, saying, 'Not now, not now. Today in the atmosphere of the country, there is a spirit of persecution, which is not that of armed force but something still more alarming because it is invisible.' "

Gandhi defended himself by accusing Tagore of preferring literature to character-building; but though he said he was sorry to think that his countrymen might follow him blindly, his words were unmeaning because he was perfectly sure that he knew best. In *Young India,* he continued to talk of nonviolence on the one hand and the joys of dying for one's country on the other. To him, indeed, there was no contradiction in these things, but his less gifted followers were easily confused.

Meanwhile, the British government of India, though uncertain and apprehensive, was not seriously shaken. Few important men gave up their professions, though among these was Motilal Nehru, a prominent lawyer closely connected with the Congress and father of Jawaharlal Nehru, later prime minister of the Indian Republic. Many students did quit school; but the "national" substitutes were unsatisfactory, and most of them began to drift back. Minor civil servants with families to support thought themselves in no position to answer Gandhi's call. But though the cry of "Swaraj in a Year" was misleading, the universal ferment was felt like the rumble of an earthquake that does not, this particular time, do great damage.

Matters came to a head in November 1920, with a visit from the Prince of Wales, which had already had to be postponed several times. Gandhi proclaimed another *hartal* to greet his arrival, and congressional organization made it effective even in the villages. In Bombay, however, when the Prince landed, there was at least a crowd to greet him, made up of rich Parsees, Jews, Eurasians, and others who did not feel included in the national effort. The consequences were violent attacks by the mob, particularly against the Parsees and Eurasians. Shops were smashed, automobiles set on fire, and policemen killed. Gandhi drove around Bombay in an automobile, vainly attempting to bring his followers, all too recognizable in *khadi* and white caps, back to their senses. He was horrified at what he saw. People dressed in foreign cloth were being beaten; Parsees were appealing to him for help; youths clad in *khadi* were massing in front of fire engines that were trying to get close to burning buildings. Worst of all, they were yelling as they saw him, "Victory to Mahatma Gandhi!" It was a nightmare.

From all over India reports came in of mob scenes on the day of the *hartal;* and Gandhi, who had beheld them with his own eyes in Bombay, was unable to hug to himself the comforting assurance that they were the fault of the British. His despair was only lightened by the news that the government, which had not hitherto applied the Rowlatt Act or interfered with the traditions of free press and free speech, was rounding up the Congress leaders for preaching sedition. He was back on familiar ground; the jails would be filled to overflowing, and prisoners cannot offer violence. Encouraged, he proceeded to plan another stage of his campaign.

The attempt to tamper with the loyalties of the Indian army had already been made by a proclamation signed by an impressive number of Muslim leaders. It had failed because on this point alone the government was swift to act and had arrested the Khilafat leaders, including the Alis. But nonpayment of taxes had yet to be tried, and it was decided that this should be started in the district of Bardoli. Accordingly, Gandhi followed his usual practice by sending an ultimatum to the Viceroy. The arrests of his followers, he declared, had made a mockery of freedom of the press and of free speech. The government must release them all and undertake in future to interfere in no way whatsoever with agitation in the country, provided that it did not take the form of violence. Since this meant violence could be openly preached and amounted to abdication by the British and installment of Gandhi as the ruler of India, the government rejected the proposal outright.

Nonpayment of taxes was scheduled to open in Bardoli on February 8, 1921. Gandhi, who had been seriously shaken by the riots in Bombay, had tried to avoid the confrontation by his ultimatum to the government, which had rejected it. Reluctantly he was being pushed toward what he could see was a decisive test. On the one hand, the peasants of Bardoli might not hold out if their possessions were sold and they themselves driven to ruin. Some have suggested that Gandhi was afraid of this outcome. It is not likely, however, that the man who led the miners of Newcastle and the peasants of Kheda would have lost his nerve.

What is far more probable is that the Bombay episode had taught him that his followers were getting out of hand. Nonpayment of taxes could not be confined to Bardoli, since all over India peasants were simmering with excitement. Bardoli must inevitably start a chain reaction that would strain the resources of the government to the utmost and might very possibly bring it to its knees. But what of India? Refusal to pay taxes must mean confrontations in every village. It would mean violence. If Gandhi could not restrain his followers in Bombay, how could he possibly control them through the length and breadth of India? What sort of revolution would it be that was ushered in by force?

Brooding over these difficulties, Gandhi was aware of other problems. His year was up, but *swaraj* was not in sight. Too many of his loyal supporters were in jail, and other helpers had fallen away. Hindu-Muslim unity was not what it had been. One result of the encouragement that had been given to fanatic ignorance by the Khilafat campaign had been the revolt of the Moplahs, a primitive Muslim tribe in South India, who had fallen on their Hindu neighbors with appalling ferocity. The massacres had served as a warning of what might happen if the passions of the people were let loose without restraint. Even more ominously, *swaraj* was not a cause that appealed to many Muslims, who saw it in terms of being ruled by a Hindu majority. They had joined the alliance because of the Khilafat and resented its being pushed aside in favor of *swaraj*.

Gandhi had set the date for the revolt of Bardoli, but only after evident misgivings. Three days earlier, on February 5, 1921, a nationalist procession had paraded past the local police station in the village of Chauri Chaura in the United Provinces. The police let it go by, but got into an argument with some stragglers. Presently the procession wheeled around, and fighting broke out. Twenty-three policemen, hopelessly outnumbered, opened fire, apparently over the heads of the crowd. After a while, their ammunition exhausted, they retired to the police station, which was set on fire. As they came rushing out, they were hacked to pieces and thrown back, living or dead, into the flames.

The episode confirmed Gandhi's worst fears. All his efforts to discipline his followers had ended in this appalling massacre. In agonies of remorse, he punished himself by a fast and called off the Bardoli campaign altogether, failing even to consult his chief lieutenants before acting.

A Quiet Recovery

THE GOVERNMENT was now free to move against Gandhi, who had at one stroke paralyzed his Hindu followers and alienated Khilafat Muslims, who found their battle lost as a result of scruples they did not share. Indeed, the ultimate effect of the great alliance was to widen the breach between Hindu and Muslim, while revealing to Muslim leaders the political power of religious fanaticism. For the moment, there was no one to make an outcry when the superintendent of police at Ahmedabad drove quietly up to Sabarmati and arrested Gandhi, equipped with a spare loincloth, seven books, and a couple of blankets.

His trial on March 18, 1922, was conducted with quiet dignity, the judge gravely bowing to the prisoner, who bowed back. Robert Broomfield, the judge, an Englishman who had spent all his active life in India, had many Indian friends and shared their admiration of Gandhi's noble ideals and saintly life. Nevertheless it was his job to carry out the law; and it had not been difficult to pick out passages from

Young India that clearly revealed Gandhi's revolutionary aims. Indeed, he had written in the simplest terms, "We want to overthrow the government. We want to *compel* its submission to the people's will."

Gandhi did not deny the charge. He went as far as the prosecution in admitting his responsibility. "It is impossible for me," he agreed, "to disassociate myself from the diabolical crimes of Chauri Chaura or the mad outrages of Bombay. He [the prosecutor] is quite right when he says that as a man of responsibility, a man having received a fair share of education, having had a fair share of experience of this world, I should have known the consequences of every one of my acts. I knew that I was playing with fire." According to his usual practice, he asked for the maximum penalty.

These were serious admissions, even though made in a spirit of defiance and accompanied by an impressive denunciation of British rule. The judge could not be accused of unfairness in sentencing him to six years in jail, but it was evident that Gandhi's behavior had restored his prestige in a way that the government was bound to find disquieting. He was removed to Yeravda prison outside Poona, while the Congress Party, as it had now become, drifted leaderless.

Gandhi was not unhappy in jail, where he was freed from the pressures of crowds. His day was carefully marked out, beginning at four o'clock when he awoke for prayer and meditation that lasted until daylight. Six hours were spent reading and writing, four hours in spinning. His reading was various, taking in Kipling, Shaw and Motley and even a novel by Jules Verne, pioneer of science fiction. People were always sending him books of a more spiritual sort, and he enjoyed these also. He was not a well-read man, having had little time for books, so that these quiet days in Yeravda were the best time he ever had for general reading. They stretched on monotonously, but he did not serve his whole sentence. In January 1924, he was stricken with appendicitis. Though successfully operated upon, he developed an abscess. The government decided to release him without conditions.

This was now an easy thing to do. The Khilafat movement had been killed by the Turkish exile of the Sultan and abolition of the Caliphate. The constitution of 1919 was working peacefully, while a formidable party in Congress, headed by Motilal Nehru and others, was anxious for Congress members to stand for election and take office so that they could protest the limitations imposed on Indian power from within the government.

With this policy Gandhi did not personally agree, but he gave way to it in order not to split the Congress party. He even suggested that he abdicate from his position of virtual dictator of Congress, so that the politically minded could run their own affairs. Congress, however, could not consent. "*Swaraj* in a Year" might have failed of its object, but it had demonstrated that the power of the masses was a vital political force that no one but Gandhi could control. Congress, therefore, faced two ways at once, supporting Motilal Nehru, yet looking to Gandhi to re-create the spirit he had conjured up in 1920.

Gandhi, convalescing slowly on the estate of a wealthy friend, found himself back at the beginning. Indeed, the situation was in some respects worse than before. The collapse of the Hindu-Muslim alliance had left feeling between Hindu and Muslim communities more strained than ever. In all of the towns and many villages, Hindu and Muslim lived close together and frequently found occasion to quarrel. The Muslims, for instance, sacrificed cows on special occasions, which gave offense to Hindus, to whom the cow is a sacred animal. Hindu festivals featured processions with noisy music which, often deliberately, went past mosques, disturbing their quiet. Any festival might be an occasion for riot, each group planning insult to the other. Nor were the grievances entirely religious, since the traditional nature of Indian occupations brought about economic differences between the groups. Thus, in a given area, the peasants might be Muslim and the moneylenders, to whom they were all in debt, entirely Hindu. Educated Muslims, who were just beginning to appear in increasing numbers, resented the monopoly of jobs by Hindus, who had for a long time possessed an educated class.

These problems, or variants of them, had existed ever since the establishment of British India. But due to the rise of Muslim and Hindu patriotism brought about by the Khilafat campaign and the nationalist movement, feelings were savagely intense. Hardly had Gandhi recovered his health before rioting broke out in the Northwest Frontier Province, where Muslims butchered Hindus and burned their houses. Gandhi could only take the sin on himself by vowing a fast for twenty-one days.

He was in Delhi, the capital; and the news of what he was doing went out all over India by newspaper, radio, and telegraph. Never had he fasted for such a long time, and it was known that he was weak. It is true that by now his fasts were carefully planned and always allowed him to sip water, mixed with bicarbonate or, in some cases, lemon juice. Nevertheless, his fast was a time of extraordinary tension, followed by Hindu-Muslim demonstrations of unity that lasted only until the next occasion for trouble. A year and a half later, for instance, his friend Swami Shraddhanand, that very Hindu leader who had been asked to preach in the mosque at Delhi on the occasion of the first *hartal*, was murdered by a Muslim fanatic as he lay ill in bed.

Gandhi regained his health very slowly. Indeed, for several years he suffered from various ailments, which he as usual tried to cure by diet. In 1927, he had a couple of slight strokes, which forced him to curtail a nationwide tour. He was fifty-eight, and it began to look as though his energies had spent themselves. It is true that he continued to preach to India; but his message concerned itself with spinning and wearing *khadi*, with Hindu-Muslim understanding, or with acceptance of the untouchables. He had coined a new name for these unfortunate people, *Harijans*, which means "Children of God"; and he never wearied of pressing their case upon the Indian public.

For about five years after his release from prison, Gandhi seemed to have abandoned his political role in favor of that of a Hindu saint and reformer. His tours of the country were still attended by such enormous crowds that his feet had to be rubbed with Vaseline after being covered with scratches from the number of people who had bowed to touch them. His message to India continued to be: "Spin daily, wear homespun, ban liquor and opium, treat Muslims as brothers, give equality to women, improve sanitation, admit the *Harijans* to your wells or temples." All such commands concerned practical acts, and it was never Gandhi's custom to criticize religious beliefs for any reason except intolerance. He was not in the philosophic sense a religious genius. He left behind him no body of new doctrine, but adapted himself to the faith of his fathers, merely reserving the right to interpret its articles in wider terms than was customary. To the Hindu, for instance, a cow is a sacred animal. It may go where it pleases, eat what it finds, and may never be slaughtered. On the other hand, it may be neglected, with the result that the miseries of India's sick or starving cows are a national scandal. Gandhi accepted the idea that the cow

Gandhi at his daily spinning

should be sacred, less on its own merits than as a reminder of man's duty to consider every living animal with respect and tenderness. Of idol-worship he could say, "I do not disbelieve," meaning that he was willing to admit that the worship of idols by others was a sincere religious act that therefore had value.

On one principle he was adamant. He accepted the role

of a Mahatma because India had forced it on him, though ruefully exclaiming, "The woes of Mahatmas are known only to Mahatmas." He would not, however, permit direct worship; he was not a god. Hinduism has many traditions of gods being incarnate in man at numerous times. Quite naturally Gandhi sometimes appeared divine to ignorant people. He met, for instance, a man who wore his picture about his neck and claimed to have been cured of paralysis by repeating, "Gandhi! Gandhi!"

"It is not I, but God who cured you," Gandhi retorted. "Will you not do me the favor of taking that photograph off your neck?"

He had always claimed that *swaraj* would come when India was spiritually ready, so that his effort during these years was really devoted to groundwork. His own spiritual state, however, was vital to his sense of fitness for the role he was trying to play. The pressure of crowds, incessant travel, the necessity of giving himself to people during every minute of his day were hard to reconcile with that detachment from the world that he desired. He took a vow of silence on Mondays, but even so he was too often forced to scribble instructions. In 1926, he vowed not to leave Sabarmati for a year. Yet from Sabarmati his articles in *Young India* came out in incessant streams, touching on birth control, religious tolerance, remarriage of child widows, and countless other matters. Despite his desire for spiritual refreshment, there was nothing of the cloudy mystic about Gandhi. He imparted no visions or divine revelations, confining himself to practical instructions intermingled with simply worded thoughts on instinct, faith or love, such as might be understood by ordinary people.

In the community of Sabarmati, Gandhi was *Bapu,* which means "Father." Kasturbai, still silently serving in the kitchen and permitted some of the attendance on her husband, was "Mother" or *Ba.* She had children and grandchildren about her. Harilal's wife had died in 1918; and the grandchildren were being brought up in Sabarmati, where their father seldom if ever visited them. As the son of a Mahatma, poor Harilal was not satisfactory. The death of Gulab seemed to have destroyed his sense of balance, and Gandhi had refused consent to his marrying again. He drifted from one job to another and in 1925 was involved in a company that, having solicited money from the public, folded up and vanished. Gandhi dissociated himself from his son in *Young India,* warning people not to invest in Harilal's projects out of respect for himself. The warning was justified; but as is usual in Gandhi's relationships with Harilal, he struck a false note, when he summed up the matter by remarking, "Men may be good, not necessarily their children."

The other sons were easier to dominate. Gandhi arranged their lives as he pleased, dispatching Manilal and Ramdas to South Africa to look after *Indian Opinion,* and refusing all of them permission to marry for as long as he could. At the age of thirty, Ramdas was finally allowed to marry a suitable girl. Devadas, though a favorite, had the misfortune to fall in love with the daughter of one of Gandhi's Congress colleagues and a close friend. The difficulty was that the girl, who returned his love, was a Brahman. Intercaste marriages were uncommon; and Gandhi, despite his work for the untouchables and his own disregard of caste rules in the interest of a higher morality, was not disposed to waive them altogether. The couple waited seven years and were finally married when Devadas was thirty-three. Manilal, unlucky enough to have attracted Gandhi's wrath by a youthful affair, was grudgingly allowed to wed at thirty-five.

Through these years Gandhi's personal life had slowly been

changing. He was still as eager to mortify his flesh and as demanding about his own or other people's lives. But physical weakness and the desire to fit his never-ending activities into the rigid framework of his day had increased his dependence on others. People gave him enemas during his fasts; they rubbed his feet or massaged him all over. Others took dictation, even while these activities were going on. They did his laundry, woke him for prayers, cooked special meals for him when he was on tour, arranged his journeys, and sat up while he slept, finishing their work. He was a hard taskmaster, always demanding that duty be perfectly done. Yet none of the people who were close to him ceased to love him, and he could still fuss kindly over his friends as he had done over Gokhale when he walked out to Tolstoy Farm in the rain and caught a cold.

The most interesting of his disciples in these years, because the most unexpected, was Mirabehn (Aunt Mira), born Madeleine Slade, the daughter of a British admiral. Unmarried and bored by the life of a daughter at home, she had long been looking for an object of devotion. For a while she thought she had found it Beethoven, for whose spirit she felt a strange affinity. Unable to play well enough to express herself, she devoted several years to arranging Beethoven concerts for a pianist who conveyed, she felt, the spirit of the master. She read a French novel written by Romain Rolland about the life of Beethoven and transferred some of her adoration to the author. Desiring to meet him, she prepared for doing so by spending a year in Paris improving her French. She gained an interview and poured out her heart. Romain Rolland, as it happened, had recently written a little book on Gandhi. Miss Slade now read it and discovered a prophet.

She wrote to Gandhi saying that she wished to join the

community at Sabarmati, but that before she did so, she would spend a year learning to spin, to speak an Indian language, to sit on the floor, and accustom herself to a vegetarian diet. Somewhat to the dismay of her family, she did all these things, made her way to Sabarmati, and became a member of the community. It was at once evident that she had accepted Gandhi as her personal god. This was in no way remarkable to him because a Hindu disciple will kiss the feet of his spiritual teacher, wait on him, and do his bidding. The relationship merely puts a responsibility on the teacher to repay this service, as it were by spiritual wages. But even Gandhi was in a certain sense dismayed by the devotion which Mirabehn poured out before him. When she was absent from him, she wrote to him every day if he would permit it; and he as teacher was obliged to answer. If he was ill, she rushed to his side, even on occasions when he had forbidden it. He was torn between admiration at the perfection of her service and a feeling that she should have a will of her own. As for Mirabehn, she was frankly puzzled,

Mirabehn with Gandhi

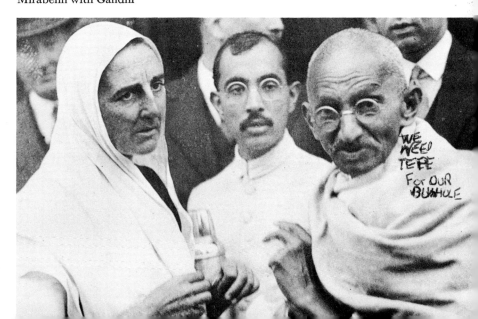

pointing out that Bapu told her to "be herself," but that when she was, her adoration tended to annoy him. Nevertheless, the relationship persisted; and Gandhi was bound to appreciate that here was somebody as convinced that he was right as he himself and only failing by a too great estimation of his merits. Among the other people at Sabarmati, Mirabehn was admired for the perfection of her devotion. There seems to have been no envy of the share that she received of Gandhi's attention, even on the part of Ba. To do her justice, Mirabehn accepted Ba as part of Gandhi and treated her with gentle understanding.

The March to the Sea

NINETEEN TWENTY-NINE had been the year fixed for the revision of the Government of India Act of 1919. By 1927, however, the Conservative government, uncertain of retaining power for another two years, saw no reason to wait and give Labour the opportunity to make a statesmanlike move. Accordingly, it appointed a parliamentary commission under Sir John Simon to go to India and investigate the problem.

The intention was excellent and the commission well chosen, but parliament had little understanding of nationalist feeling. Congress was now demanding the right for India to choose her own constitution, be it Dominion status, independence, or some transitional system. The appointment of a commission without any Indians on it struck them as an insult. Not only did Congress members refuse to testify before it, but they organized demonstrations wherever it came, displaying black flags and chanting the slogan, "Simon, go home!" Under these difficulties the commission accomplished little, while the Viceroy, Lord Irwin, whose liberal-conservative Indian advisers had pressed him not to admit any Indians to the commission lest it become the tool of faction, looked on aghast.

Not to be outdone by the commission, Congress appointed its own committee under Motilal Nehru to draw up a constitution for independent India. This served to emphasize the fact that though Gandhi and Congress claimed to speak for the whole of India, they did not actually do so. Thinking of itself as an all-India group because it contained a number of Muslims, Congress did not thrash out problems with the Muslim League, an organization that was beginning to assume political importance. Its ablest member, Mohammed Ali Jinnah, was abroad at the time that the Nehru committee was doing its work and returned only after its report was issued. He hastened to sabotage Motilal's work by demanding fourteen changes that not merely gave electoral favors to Muslims, but insisted that no bill could ever be passed if three quarters of the delegates of any special community group were against it.

By 1930, there was complete estrangement between Congress and the Muslim League, and also between Congress and England. This feeling was intensified throughout the country by the economic effects of the worldwide depression. Gandhi signified his return to the political arena by leading the peasants of Bardoli in a refusal to pay their taxes unless they were reduced. This resulted in a campaign conducted by the peasants with extraordinary restraint and ending in a negotiated victory. Gandhi had good reason to think that the work of the last five years had readied India to make another attempt at nonviolent resistance.

The government's answer, at the suggestion of Lord Irwin, was a round-table conference between Indians and British in London in order to work out some definite proposals for the next stage in Indian self-government. Congress, however, refused to participate, claiming that as sole representatives of the independence movement, they alone had any right to be consulted. On the twenty-sixth of January, 1930, Gandhi announced a Declaration of Independence, calling on his followers to hoist the national flag.

His plans were taking shape for a new campaign of *Satyagraha,* behind which, thanks to the reorganization of Congress, he could expect to have the better part of a million workers who were responsive to instructions from the top. He himself for the last five years had been preaching to the people on hand spinning, love of one's neighbor, and the peaceful gospel of *Satyagraha.* Thus with his meaning more widely understood and his followers better disciplined, he could make preparations for renewing the struggle.

This time he gave much thought to choosing a form of protest that could appeal to Indians at every level. Carefully he drew up a list of grievances, including items that should appeal to the economic difficulties of businessmen, such as the demand for revaluation of the rupee together with an attack on the land tax and other things that were popular with the peasants. Unjust taxes had long been a part of his complaint against the British. Strangely enough, he did not criticize them for taxing the poor rather than the rich; and the great industrialists among his supporters were never troubled by a hint of socialism. Truth was, he did not believe in government. His ideas of social services were those that men render voluntarily to their neighbors. Revenue, for instance, did not mean more funds for education to Gandhi; he thought of it in terms of the Indian army and the upkeep of a government bureaucracy that he considered expensive. The plight of the poor was always close to his heart, and so he criticized the paying of taxes.

Apart from the land or real-estate tax, there were two taxes that especially roused his indignation: the liquor tax and the salt tax. The liquor tax was, to his mind, making money out of the degradation of other people. He was, in fact, an ardent prohibitionist; whereas the British, perceiving that the ingredients of alcohol were available everywhere, preferred to control it by taxing as steeply as they dared without creating a flourishing black market. Thus part of any Gandhi campaign, and in particular the one he was now planning, would be the picketing of liquor shops.

The salt tax was in another category. Salt was a government monopoly and sold to the public at a slight government profit. A salt tax, like a head tax, presses equally on everyone, whether he be rich or poor. It is true that the tax was exceedingly low and the salt was free from impurities; but in parts of India, particularly on some of the beaches, salt was free for the taking and could have been purified, at least somewhat, by the villagers themselves. Thus by manufacturing and selling salt, demonstrators could fill the jails in typical Gandhi fashion, while engaging in an occupation that would bring tiny profits to poor people and be more popular with them than the hawking of forbidden pamphlets that none of them could read.

Once resistance to the salt tax had been decided on, Gandhi needed a symbolic action to dramatize the campaign and lift it up into the sight of all. The solution was simple and typical of Gandhi. On the morning of March 12, 1930, he set out at the head of a band of volunteers to walk from Sabarmati to the seashore at Dandi, 241 miles off, to gather salt.

It was in essence quite a small procession led by a little man of sixty-one in a loincloth, stepping briskly out on matchstick legs and somewhat bowed forward as he helped himself along with a bamboo staff. Behind him walked seventy-nine of his disciples; and behind them rumbled a bullock cart, provided by anxious admirers in case the old man's strength should break down. Ahmedabad came out to see him off in a procession two miles long and strewed his path with green leaves. Reporters from all the Indian papers and a number of foreign correspondents straggled behind, each wiring home stories from the villages he passed. Gandhi was in no hurry; and he stopped everywhere long enough to urge the people to use the spinning wheel, treat untouchables as brothers, improve sanitation, give up alcohol, and break the salt monopoly. As in 1920, he could arouse a feeling that India must soon burst its bonds, that independence was a matter of a few months. In his wake village headmen resigned their posts, leaving their people without representatives to deal with government officials. *Swaraj* was coming, and it did not matter.

It was very hot, so that Gandhi only marched ten or fifteen miles a day, calling frequent halts. This pilgrimage was to be made on his own terms; and he ordered his followers to reject the milk and fruits that were sent from a distance and to rely on the poor provisions of the villages. The Viceroy, he pointed out, received an income four thousand times as great as the average Indian. His own followers were of a different sort, as they must show by living off the country.

Lord Irwin's government held its hand for twenty-four days while the march slowly neared its objective. Irritating though it might be to the Viceroy to see the newspapers of the world entranced by the picture of a half-naked old man taking on the British Empire, still Gandhi had not yet broken the salt law. Irwin did so far forget himself as to hope that Gandhi would die of a stroke on the road, but this solution was not granted him. At Dandi, everything had been meticulously prepared, even down to the date of the ceremony, which coincided with that of the massacre of Amritsar. After a whole night of prayer, Gandhi and his followers waded into the sea for a bath of purification. Then before the lines of spectators, he walked over to the caked salt left by evaporation and picked up a little piece, which was later sold at auction for sixteen hundred rupees. There were no policemen present, and the quiet that followed the act was an anticlimax.

Within a week, India had exploded. Everyone had to make salt, picket liquor shops, light bonfires of foreign cloth, or annoy the government. The leaders of Congress, many of whom had tended to pooh-pooh the salt idea, were frantically busy producing leaflets with drawings of salt pans and instructions. It was exciting; it was impressive; but was it revolution? Enthusiasm burned brightly; the mobs were out again in the cities. While Gandhi was thinking over his next move, the British government faced its first serious threat and acted firmly.

Around Peshawar on the northwest frontier, Abdul Gaffar Khan, a remarkable man known as the "frontier Gandhi" had established an organization among the warlike Muslim tribes of the area, whom he clad in red shirts and formed into an "army" devoted to pacifist principles and service. Long one of the prominent Muslim supporters of Gandhi, he swung his organization into line with the national movement. For all his peaceful principles, Gaffar Khan controlled turbulent tribes; and the authorities in Peshawar thought the situation was getting ugly. They arrested him and lodged him in jail. Demonstrations in protest could not even be controlled by armored cars. The police abandoned Peshawar to the mob, which released Gaffar Khan and took control of the city. Three days later, a couple of platoons of regular soldiers, in this case Hindus, were sent into Peshawar to restore order. But they refused to fire on the Muslim crowd and broke their ranks. The British had to send a detachment with air support to retake the city.

This incident served a grave warning on the British government. Once the loyalty of troops cannot be relied on, any government is at an end. The Viceroy, anxious to prevent the disastrous news from getting about, clamped censorship on the Indian press, forbidding further mention of the civil disobedience movement. Gandhi was furious. By this time sixty thousand of his supporters had been arrested for breach of the laws, while in various confrontations between authorities and rioters, shots had been fired and people killed. He did not want another Chauri Chaura, but he was angry enough to say in advance and before the thing was on his conscience that he washed his hands of it. If the government by repressive measures drove the Indian people to desperation, let the blood of its servants be on the government's head.

It is fair to say that in the clashes between resisters and the police, it was usually Gandhi's forces that suffered casualties or unnecessarily brutal treatment. There was bound to be some popular violence, particularly in the towns, where criminal gangs were only too ready to make profit out of a disordered situation. But Gandhi's confidence in the people was on the whole not misplaced. There was no Chauri Chaura, no Bombay riot, no Moplah rising. His power over the masses, reinforced by the last years of quiet work, was able to stave off the threat of pure anarchy that had troubled him in 1922.

In any case, Gandhi deliberately intended more blood to flow, but of his own followers. He wanted to force the government into an outrage that would whip up feeling and reveal the British in an unenviable light. Accordingly, he made plans to take over the government-owned Dharasana saltworks through a massive invasion of unarmed *Satyagrahis*. As usual, he announced his intentions; but by now the government, alarmed by events at Peshawar, had decided to face the troubles that would follow his arrest and get them over. The actual details had been as carefully planned as the secret interview with General Smuts in Pretoria. Gandhi was roused out of sleep to be taken by a combination of special railroad coach and closed automobile to Yeravda, where he was confined at the government's pleasure under a statute passed in 1825 that everybody had considered obsolete. This time the British did not dare to stage a trial.

Since it was always Gandhi's practice to arrange for leadership, should he be arrested, the raid on the saltworks was carried out on schedule under command of the poetess, Mrs. Sarojini Naidu. It was a place situated on a barren coast and protected by a barbed-wire fence, in front of which there was a drainage ditch. Four hundred policemen under six British officers had been posted between the barbed wire and the ditch with instructions to hold the place at any cost. They were armed with *lathis*, bamboo staffs with metal tips, their standard weapons. Behind them on a little knoll were twenty-five native riflemen; for the government, like Gandhi, had seen this as a battle that could decide between British rule and anarchy. Any surrender would bring take-overs in every place, followed by revolution.

The raiders approaching under Mrs. Naidu consisted of some twenty-five hundred people clad in the white "Gandhi" forage cap, with homespun shirts and *dhotis*. This human tide flowed up to the edge of the ditch, all shouting, "Long live the revolution!" at the tops of their voices. They crossed in detachments, some of them carrying ropes to help scale

Mrs. Sarojini Naidu walks with Gandhi to the shore at Dandi to gather salt

the barbed wire. As soon as they were over the ditch, the police fell on them with their *lathis* and clubbed them down. Not one so much as lifted his hand to protect his head as the sickening sound of bamboo clubs on skulls and collarbones was heard by the spectators, among whom was Webb Miller, an American journalist.

People collapsed, groaning and squirming or unconscious; but the first detachment was followed unhesitatingly by another, then another, attempting to overwhelm the police by sheer weight of numbers. The stretcher-bearers, making their way through the confusion, collected the injured in blankets that were soon soaked in blood.

No orders were given the troops to fire; but the policemen, struggling for two hours with overwhelming masses at a temperature of a hundred and sixteen degrees in the shade, appeared to have gone crazy. People were deliberately kicked as they lay on the ground or subjected to indignities that clearly amounted to torture. Meanwhile, a little shed with a thatched roof that afforded protection from the burning sun was taken over for a field hospital; and hundreds of groaning people were laid down in or near it.

After two hours, it was all over. In a sense the raid had failed, but in another it had served its purpose well. Between British and Indian there lay a second shadow, darkening Amritsar. Webb Miller, his indignation vivid in his words, published the treatment of unarmed, unresisting men in articles that were echoed all over the world. According to the Congress report, two people died of their injuries, while two hundred and ninety suffered serious wounds. Through the genius of Gandhi, both victory and defeat strengthened his cause.

Round Table Conference

THE APPOINTMENT of Lord Irwin as viceroy of India in 1926 had seemed a statesmanlike gesture. An able, though not a brilliant politician, he was to have a distinguished career after succeeding to his father's title of Lord Halifax. In 1940, Halifax was actually considered for prime minister instead of Churchill; and he later served as foreign minister in Churchill's Cabinet and as war ambassador to the United States. By 1926 he had already taken the opportunity to show his sympathy with the subject races of the British Empire, while his own deep religious convictions gave him understanding of Gandhi's. Unquestionably Irwin had hoped to bring Indians together and to preside over the establishment of a reformed constitution. Instead, he found himself forced to muzzle the press, put a hundred thousand people in jail, expose his government to critical reports in foreign papers, and detain Gandhi without trial on the authority of an act that was only dubiously valid.

Lord Irwin contemplated this position without joy. As

soon as all members of the Congress Working Committee were behind bars, he attempted to negotiate with Gandhi. For this purpose he arranged an important meeting in Yeravda jail, bringing Motilal Nehru and his son, Patel, and several others to meet Gandhi in the hope that they would consent to a compromise. This committee proved adamant; its only terms were complete independence, and the only points it would discuss were the mechanics of the Indian take-over. Irwin had to wait until agitation had spent its force a few months later. He then released the leaders unconditionally, though too late for Motilal Nehru, who was already an old man and worn out by his exertions in the campaign, followed by imprisonment. He died a few days after his release, while Gandhi, who had been restrained by his influence from negotiations with Irwin, soon became more approachable.

Lord Irwin accordingly won the consent of Gandhi to a series of discussions that took place in the Viceroy's study. The two opponents made a curious contrast. Gandhi, huddled in a shawl and warming his thin legs by the Viceroy's fire, had shrunk with age so that he now looked tiny. His head was shaved and nearly bald; he had lost his front teeth, while his bat-ears stuck out as far as ever. His bright eyes were concealed behind a pair of gold-rimmed spectacles. The Viceroy, facing him in an armchair, was six-foot five, lean and solemn-looking, with a high domed head and ears as prominent as Gandhi's. He had little reason to like Gandhi, who had destroyed all that he had set out to do for India; but he was still attracted by the sincerity of the man and understood his outlook better than most English political figures were able to do.

Conversations went on for several days. Irwin's secretary

later made the comment that the Viceroy showed commendable patience because Gandhi, who had grown to like the sound of his own voice, kept launching into lectures that were not to the point. This is an interesting reflection on Gandhi because it gives a portrait not of the saint, but of the person. Here is the little man who must have his way, but must get it by persuasion. Since to Gandhi truth was simple, he never could see that some men were not persuadable, among them Lord Irwin. Representative of Britain's best intentions toward India and knowing in detail the difficulties of carrying these out, the Viceroy could not be convinced that British rule was purely evil. Gandhi's eagerness to prevail was heightened by a sense of grievance that burst out, relevant or not. To be correct, he had at least a hundred thousand grievances, for the fate of each man who had been arrested was a separate cause for resentment. By this time, the heat of the struggle had affected his own attitude. He had come to believe that breaking the law in a nonviolent way should go unpunished. He had to express all these feelings, and Irwin was forced to listen.

Despite their differences, each could respect the other. Irwin's proposal was that Gandhi should call off his campaign for the present and go to London to thrash out constitutional problems at the Round Table Conference, where non-Congress Indians were already demanding self-government. In return, Irwin would release all *Satyagrahis* who were not concerned in crimes of violence and would return fines that had been already levied. Gandhi wanted an inquiry into police brutality, but the Viceroy insisted that it would aggravate ill feeling and that there had been faults on both sides. When Gandhi persisted, Irwin, as he reports, broke out with perfect frankness:

Finally I said that I would tell him the main reason why I could not give him what he wanted. I had no guarantee that he might not start civil disobedience again, and if and when he did, I wanted the police to have their tails up and not down. Whereupon his face lit up and he said, "Ah, now Your Excellency treats me like General Smuts treated me in South Africa. You do not.deny that I have an equitable claim, but you advance unanswerable reasons from the point of view of the government why you cannot meet it. I drop the demand."

The quality here shown could make friends out of Gandhi's opponents, but it caused some supporters to comment that in negotiations he tended to throw away a position of advantage.

The treaty worked out between Gandhi and Lord Irwin became known as the Delhi Pact because it was ratified by a meeting of the Congress held at Delhi. It offered both sides a chance to cool off while constitutional questions were discussed in London. But Congress, which had previously demanded the largest representation in the conference, now made the mistake of electing Gandhi as its sole delegate. In this way it entrusted the political future of India to a man whose views were essentially nonpolitical, while depriving the conference of other Congress members who might have had a powerful influence upon it. Still claiming to represent all nationalist India, Congress was not anxious to bargain for power with other Indians who were of a different mind. In general it felt that nothing would come of the conference unless the old magician could work a miracle. Perhaps Gandhi felt this, too. At all events he consented to an arrangement that was unlikely to produce a positive result.

This decision was a poor start to the new truce, and nothing afterward went very well. There were endless petty squabbles about the implementation of the Delhi Pact. Lord Willingdon, who had just replaced Irwin, was a genial man, experienced both in the problems of India and in those of his office, popular with rajahs, and indeed with everyone who personally knew him, but far from willing to grant interviews to Gandhi, who had a weakness for going to the top about trivial matters.

Gandhi finally boarded the boat for England with seven companions, outraged to discover that his attendants had accepted all sorts of presents from friends, both for his comfort and for their own. Inspecting everybody's luggage, he had all the extras shipped back from Aden. He arrived in England in the rain of a British September in a loincloth, woollen shawl, and sandals. Henry Polak, his old friend from South African days, had arranged for him to stay in a settlement house in Bow, a slum quarter down near the docks that offered congenial hospitality but was a long way from the scene of the conference. Presently Gandhi was forced to rent a flat in Knightsbridge, where his three secretaries could work, and where he could see people. Transport between here and his sleeping quarters in Bow complicated a day that was already cumbered with prayers starting at four A.M., a brisk walk of an hour between six and seven, and the daily spinning quota. Gandhi almost never got to bed before midnight, and frequently later. Not unnaturally, he closed his eyes during the long political discussions of the conference, which did not interest him, leaving Congress without the active participation of any member in such matters.

He demanded no more from himself than he did from others. He had brought Madeleine Slade as his personal attendant with the kindly intention of giving her a chance

to see her family. He seems to have given no thought to the slightly shocked sensation with which London society saw the daughter of a distinguished admiral serving him on her knees and bowing low to kiss his feet. Nor did Mirabehn have much time for social life. It was her duty to set her alarm for ten minutes to four in order to wake Gandhi up on the stroke of the hour. She joined his prayers and then, while he slept for an hour, she took a briefer nap, again rising early to wake him with a morning drink of hot water, honey, and lemon. She accompanied him on the brisk walk, on return from which she heated his bath water, provided his breakfast, and saw him off in the government car, snatching intervals for her own toilet. She cleaned their rooms, made a bundle of his and her discarded clothes for washing, bought provisions, cooked and packed his midday meal and, carrying this in one hand and the washing bundle in the other, set off by subway for the Knightsbridge office, a journey that took Gandhi forty-five minutes in the government car. Arriving, she washed the clothes by hand and hung them out in hopes that they would dry before the evening. She served Gandhi lunch if he were back, or gave the basket to one of the others to take to him, or took it herself. She prepared and served the evening meal and worked in the office, returning to the settlement house by subway at eight or nine o'clock to await Gandhi's arrival, which was probably between eleven and twelve. She then gave him his spinning and afterward put him to sleep by rubbing his feet, which must always have been cold in the English climate. Much of her endless day could clearly have been shortened, had Gandhi not insisted on living precisely as he did in India, availing himself of the government car, but not permitting cars to Mirabehn or spending Congress money on a laundress. Principle to him was more important than convenience.

Gandhi arriving in England for the Round Table Conference

Meanwhile, Gandhi was concerned with much more than the conference. He had by now many English admirers, with the help of whom he set himself to win over the hearts of people in England. Almost no audience was refused, whether cotton spinners in Manchester, professors at Oxford, newspaper editors, the Secretary of State for India, or Charlie Chaplin. In fact, the only invitation that caused him to hesitate was one to an official party given by King George V and Queen Mary for the Indian delegation. This presented a delicate question because he had renounced his allegiance to that monarch and had declared that India was independent. However, as a guest of England he decided that he ought to accept, though he politely rejected a suggestion from the Lord Chamberlain that he wear a little more costume.

The party took place and proved to be a richly comic occasion. King George V had been married and a father before Queen Victoria died. His ideas of kingship had been formed in an old-fashioned school. He was a blunt man with a strong sense of duty that included not only his duty to his people but that of his people to him. Forthright and uncomprehending, he lectured Gandhi about stirring up trouble in "my" Empire and agitating "my" people. "I won't have it," the King said.

"Your Majesty must not expect me to argue the point," answered Gandhi, annoyed by the situation and contemptuous of the King. He stole the chance to have the last word later when someone asked him if he had not been embarrassed by appearing at the party in his well-worn shawl and cotton loincloth. "The King had on enough for both of us," he retorted.

The delegates to the Round Table Conference had been carefully chosen to include representatives of every minority group. Among them were princes, untouchables, Sikhs, Muslims, Christians, Hindus, Parsees, landowners, union leaders, and presidents of chambers of commerce. No one had been found to represent the peasants, who, though they formed the majority of Indians, were so divided in outlook that it proved impossible to select among them. With this important exception, every interest that the British thought they ought to protect was included, with the natural result that an agreement on anything was difficult to obtain. It is true that, to the surprise of the government, even the princes had agreed in the previous session that self-rule and a federation of the whole subcontinent were essential for India. It was this decision that had given the conference a fresh lease on life and had led to Gandhi's consenting to attend the second session.

Unfortunately, it proved easier to agree on the general principle than on details. If the British, as the Congress later accused them of doing, had chosen the delegates with the intention of setting them one against another, they could hardly have done better. Something might have been achieved if the government had put forward concrete proposals that could have been the subject of debate, but after the fate of the Simon Commission at Indian hands, this was too much to expect.

In this situation, Gandhi was not helpful. From the start he claimed that Congress represented eighty-five percent of the Indian people. This merely infuriated Muslim delegates, who feared Congress as largely Hindu, and it also offended the princes, since it implied that their subjects recognized the Congress as a higher authority. Gandhi's calm assumption that he represented the untouchables because of his work on their behalf maddened Dr. Ambedkar, who actually was an untouchable and despised Gandhi for trying to solve

Gandhi seated among the delegates at the Round Table Conference

the problem by appealing to the conscience of caste Hindus. Ambedkar wanted action backed up by definite laws that were calculated to raise the untouchables out of poverty and ignorance. Thus the divisions that troubled the conference were actually increased by the presence of Gandhi.

His attitude to the problems of the Indian take-over was equally negative. The Muslims and the British liberals were substantially in agreement that defense and external relations should be managed by the Viceroy during a transitional period. Congress, on the other hand, had instructed its delegation to work for immediate control over defense, foreign affairs, finance, and so forth, subject to any adjustments that were necessary in the interests of India. Gandhi, taking the first part of this resolution as an absolute mandate, refused to compromise anywhere. He had no suggestions as to how an Indian government could control the Indian army without any period of transitional arrangement. He merely repeated that all matters should be left to the Indian people, who would settle them as they pleased. "The iceberg of communal differences," as he put it, "will melt under the warmth of the sun of freedom." Meanwhile, he himself on the minorities subcommittee could bring about no agreement on minority rights.

All this in itself was enough to destroy the conference, but the British government had also lost interest in giving outright freedom to India. A Liberal-Labour combination that supported Lord Irwin had consented to the conference. They had aroused antagonism from right-wing Conservatives, who proved able to press their point of view on the Conservative Party. During the conference, the Labour government fell and was replaced by a coalition that was, except in name, Conservative. If the Indian delegation had been able to settle its differences, it is just possible that the new government might have given way; but its interest in making radical changes was certainly waning. Gandhi and the Congress always heatedly accused the British of fostering divisions in order to keep themselves in power. If that is slightly less than fair, it was at least true that, as a Muslim leader put it: "It is the old maxim of divide and rule. But there is a division of labor here. *We* divide, and *you* rule." The disputes of the conference were held by the new British leaders to be less a tragedy than an opportunity.

The Children of God

By THE TIME Gandhi returned to India at the end of December 1931, Lord Willingdon, the Viceroy, had made up his mind how to act. Since the Round Table Conference had been fruitless, it was to be expected that Gandhi and Congress would embark on a new campaign of nonviolent resistance. Lord Willingdon, pondering the mistakes of Irwin, had no intention of allowing the nationalists to make plans and set affairs in motion before he took any action to prevent them. He preferred, in other words, to set up a police state rather than to endure another rebellion. Accordingly, he had already arrested Nehru and various other Congress leaders before Gandhi landed in Bombay to face a tumultuous welcome. Nor would he grant Gandhi an interview, preferring to have him taken back to Yeravda jail within the week.

Gandhi submitted quietly. He had Patel and Mahadev Desai with him, while the government, recognizing that he was detained without a trial, allowed him many special privileges. He could write, for instance, and receive all the letters that he wanted, though everything that went or came was censored. Many visitors were allowed to see him, and his regular routine took up much time. He had leisure to meditate over the lessons of the Round Table Conference, and by March he had made up his mind sufficiently to write a long letter to Sir Samuel Hoare, Secretary of State for India.

The failure of the Round Table Conference to reach agreement had not altered the necessity of reviewing the Government of India Act of 1919. It had merely left the British government to decide what it would grant and what recommendations of what particular groups in the conference it would favor. Prominent among these in Gandhi's mind was the question that had divided himself and Dr. Ambedkar on the minorities' subcommittee. Ambedkar insisted that the untouchables should have a certain number of representatives in the assemblies at provincial or national level who should be elected solely by untouchables. Gandhi replied that this would perpetuate the very division that it was his ambition to destroy. Brooding over the question, he was coming around to the conclusion that it would be intolerable to drive this wedge between the castes and the outcastes. Hinduism, if it meant anything, must be united. Accordingly, his letter to Sir Samuel contained the threat that if the British considered favorably Dr. Ambedkar's motion, he might commence a fast until he died.

It was a step that did not commend itself to his own friends and followers, including Nehru, who was appalled that the old man should try to get his way on a political arrangement by blackmail. Nor did the British government, after considering the matter, yield to coercion. Its decision was not published for several months; but when it came, it favored Ambedkar.

By this time, Gandhi had leisure to examine his own motives, which had not satisfied him entirely either, and to lift the issue onto a higher plane. In August, he announced his firm resolution to begin his fast on the twentieth of September, which was about a month away. Gradually it dawned on Nehru as it did on India that the fast represented a protest, not solely against Dr. Ambedkar, but against the continuance of the whole outcaste system.

By now a Gandhi fast was a solemn rite ushered in by prayers and attended by a bevy of doctors and newspaper correspondents. While he was strong enough to talk, he would assure everybody that water would prolong life a

Gandhi taking his last meal before a fast

long time and that he would not easily let go. All the same, he was now well over sixty; and the doctors feared lest paralysis set in, or lest he reach a condition from which even food would not help him recover.

An extraordinary effort was made by Gandhi's friends, permitted by the government to gather in Yeravda, to draft a compromise permitting a primary election in which only untouchables should vote, which should elect a number of candidates for each untouchable seat. They would then run against one another in a general election. The details were highly technical, and Dr. Ambedkar took time to argue them out. When an agreement was finally reached, it had to be presented to the British Cabinet in London, calling the Prime Minister away from attending a funeral and causing him to sit up until midnight over a discussion about whether the arrangement could be accepted.

By now the first week of Gandhi's fast was ending. To begin with he had suffered from nausea, vomiting, and painful cramps; but these had passed. He could no longer walk or sit up and had to be helped to turn over in bed. The doctors were afraid he would sink into a coma. But India, as well as the politicians, had got the point of his message. Everywhere temples were being flung open to outcastes; they were walking down highways and drawing water from public wells. Many people were joining them in ceremonial meals. There were extraordinary scenes as doors were opened and Gandhi's "Children of God" came in for the first time.

By the twenty-seventh, Gandhi's bed had been carried into the shade of a mango tree in the prison yard. Only a few people were allowed near him, among them India's other great man, Rabindranath Tagore. Little was said, for though Gandhi could still speak, the effort tired him. At four o'clock that afternoon the inspector general of prisons entered the courtyard with the long-awaited agreement, now officially approved by London. Gandhi's friends held their breath as he read it slowly. Would he consider it satisfactory or not? He was uncertain and suggested consultation with Ambedkar, thinking there was time for another conference. His friends, who knew better, tactfully pointed out that further discussion would probably open up another breach. Doubtfully he gave way. The courtyard was hastily purified by sprinkling water, and two hundred people who had crowded outside to hear the news were admitted. A Bengali hymn was sung and some Sanskrit verses chanted before Kasturbai, who had been rushed to Yeravda some days earlier, handed Gandhi a glass of orange juice. The fast was broken.

Dr. Ambedkar, a plain and practical man, was frankly puzzled by the entire episode, pointing out that Gandhi had conceded special seats for the *Harijans* even if their candidates were to run in a general election. Had he been willing to commit himself at the Round Table Conference, the whole arrangement might have been worked out in an orderly fashion. Ambedkar did not see, as Gandhi did, that a mere compromise would not have been honored by the Hindu masses. Gandhi had needed his special form of blackmail to create the climate in which nothing mattered but saving his life. It is fair to say that as soon as this tremendous week was over, Indian consciences sank back to rest. Many temples were closed again, and in the country districts *Harijans* sank back into the position of outcastes. Eventually, however, untouchability was doomed. Congress now saw this, and the country at large had agreed. Generations might go by before a position hallowed by the custom of centuries could be forgotten, but Gandhi had settled the question of its ultimate future as no one else in India could have done.

Yeravda jail sank back to normal with instructions that

Gandhi's visitors were to be cut off and that he was to be treated as a prisoner, not an honored guest or a dying patient. He was still a privileged prisoner, however. Brooding over the untouchables, he decided that a newspaper dealing with their plight might help to change opinions. The government, delighted to have him occupy himself with a nonpolitical reform, consented to allow him to write lead articles from prison. But even the publication of *Harijan* could not satisfy Gandhi. The sin of Hinduism lay heavy on his conscience, so that in May 1933, he began a fast of twenty-one days in penance for it.

Once more friends were appalled. A week had nearly killed him, and twenty-one days was simple suicide. The government shared their opinion and did not want him to die on their hands. Hastily they released him, and he was hurried to a luxurious mansion in which to undergo his ordeal with friends about him. Amazingly, he survived and bent his powers of concentration to the task of getting well, obeying the doctors for once and sipping endless glasses of goat's milk.

During all the time that he had been in Yeravda, he had been managing Sabarmati from a distance, interfering as usual with the minutest details, decreeing, for instance, that every house should have a notice on it stating when it had last been cleaned and when it was due for cleaning again. But Sabarmati had become a problem. Not only did it house over a hundred people, but it was well equipped with fields and workshops valuable both in themselves and as a source of income. The government had assessed it for taxes, which Gandhi would not pay. Accordingly, when taxes were overdue the government seized property equivalent to what was owing. This recurring situation had greatly increased the problem of management. Gandhi was forced to consider what he ought to do, and his final solution was to simplify his life once more. He decided to abandon Sabarmati and break it up.

He used the occasion for another demonstration against the government, planning a march with the inmates in order to court arrest. But he was seized before he could set out, imprisoned briefly, and released under an order not to leave Poona. Disobeying, he was arrested once more and sentenced to another year in jail.

Back in Yeravda, Gandhi was refused permission to continue his work for the untouchables. The government saw no reason to permit him to enjoy the limelight, so long as he would not agree to give up political agitation. Once more he resorted to a fast to the death. When it was thought that he was actually dying, the government released him. Amazingly, he came back to life again and was removed to Wardha, the community of Vinoba Bhave, the disciple who had heard Gandhi speak in Benares in front of Mrs. Besant, and who had followed him ever since. Less than three months after his release, the indomitable old man undertook a pilgrimage that lasted nearly a year, covering India to speak for the Harijans, to open the doors of temples to them, to raise money for them from jewelry donated him by women, and always to appeal to men's compassionate hearts.

It was hard work, the more so because for the first time he was opposed by his own tactics. A band of orthodox Hindus practiced passive resistance against him, lying down in front of the temples to keep the doors from being opened or massing in front of Gandhi's hut to keep him inside. There were also violent acts. His car was stoned, and in Poona a bomb was thrown which hit the wrong car and injured seven people.

He had recovered his health, but all was not well with him.

The Wardha community, which he had by now remodeled to his liking, was another Sabarmati. Congress members, pilgrims, disciples, newspaper men came there incessantly. Some years earlier he had taken the vow to observe a day of silence on Mondays, but even so he had to write answers or instructions. There was no rest anywhere. He had officially abdicated from control of Congress; but nothing went on without his advice, so that actually he was as busy as before with political decisions.

He had told his friends from Sabarmati to go and live in villages alongside the peasants, establishing cottage industries and better sanitation, preaching fair treatment of the untouchables and other reforms. In a passion for simplicity, he had even sent Mirabehn from him, though he could not do without attendants as long as his life was so confused. He told Mirabehn to find him a place to build a hut at Segaon, the village where she was living not far from Wardha. In the meantime he would live in the open there with a bamboo matting to protect him against the sun.

In this fashion Gandhi came to Segaon to establish himself in an empty field, deliberately choosing a spot remote from roads and post offices. But even Segaon proved useless as a refuge. Presently a road had to be built and telegraph wires strung. He needed people about him as much as before. Then too, he could not refuse those who appealed to him. Segaon became transformed to Sevagram, "Service Village." It went on very much like Sabarmati, except for the fact that a real village of six hundred ordinary peasants was also available for Gandhi's teaching and preaching. He had tried to retreat from the world, but still it came to him.

It is hard to say how much he was affected during this unsettled time by the never-ending problem of Harilal, his oldest son. By this time Harilal seemed to have lost any purpose, save that of tormenting his father by making his own life a public scandal. His affairs with women had been many. He was a drunkard and had sunk to tramping the roads or riding the railways, turning up from time to time to borrow money from his brothers or his son, to whom he still showed remnants of great charm. To Gandhi he would write abusive letters when he was drunk, accusing him of being a tyrant and a false Mahatma. Harilal was news to the papers, and the use of his name was worth money to those who had dubious schemes to promote. In vain did his father warn the public not to trust him. Eventually, it got about that Harilal might be persuaded to change his faith; and unscrupulous people from several religions made offers that amounted to outright bribery. On one of his rare visits, he boasted to Gandhi that all the fools were after him, though actually he was a devout student of the *Gita*. Perhaps he was trying out his father's reaction, for his desire to hurt Gandhi seems to have been even stronger than the temptation of money. For whatever reason, in May 1936, he entered the Muslim faith in a public ceremony in Bombay, assuming the name of Abdullah Gandhi.

The conversion was meant to ridicule his father, and it succeeded. Muslim bitterness against Hindus was rising in the 1930s, and there were plenty who were willing to parade their disreputable convert with mock solemnity. Never one to leave well enough alone, Gandhi printed a long letter to his "numerous Muslim friends" in the pages of *Harijan*, giving approval to any genuine religious conversion, but plainly stating that Harilal's was false.

Gandhi certainly felt the blow, but he was able to put it down to Harilal's having been "conceived in sin" as a result of his own too-early marriage. Kasturbai, on the other hand, had no such resource and was shocked by Harilal's abandonment of Hindu traditions, which were part of her whole life. She dictated a letter to Harilal full of bitter reproach and, beneath it all, of love. "And often when I have sleepless nights I think of you and wonder where you are these days, what you are eating, where you are staying, etc. . . . But even if any time I chanced to meet you, I am afraid you might insult me." In many ways poor Kasturbai had a hard life.

It was not until 1935 that the British government was ready with a Government of India Act to replace the one that had been introduced in 1919. Despite all the mistakes that had been made and the little sympathy that existed between the Conservative Party and Congress, the act of 1935 was a creditable attempt to give self-government to India. It provided for a federation between the eleven British provinces, which were now to become completely self-governing, and the 605 princely states. The central Parliament, chosen by a complicated system designed to give fair representation to everyone, was to have all the powers of a federal government save those of foreign relations and defense. Even these were after a few years of transition to be given over into Indian hands. In fact, the object of the act, as clearly stated, was to transfer power in an orderly fashion to an independent government of India within the empire.

The only difficulty with the arrangement of 1935 was that it did not work. The princes, who had at the Round Table called for federation, had by this time developed doubts about their chances of survival amid a sea of self-governing Indian provinces. The new constitution was in fact a concession made from an English point of view and dedicated to protecting the minority groups that divided India. Without the princes there could be no federation, so that it proved impossible to put the act in force. The provinces, however, could govern themselves and might possibly hope to persuade the princes in the long run. Congress in consequence had to make up its mind whether it would permit its members to stand for election in their various provinces, backing them as an organized party in the hope of taking over provincial governments.

There was hot debate about this matter in Congress. On the one hand, the nationalists had not got what they wanted, a completely free India under Congress's sway. A federation that could only be had by approval of the princes and did not immediately govern the army or foreign affairs was unsatisfactory. But on the other hand, if Congress continued to abstain from cooperation and took no part in provincial government, other groups would fill the gap. Other people would gain administrative powers, form parties, and get used to being at the head of affairs. With practical politicians like Patel and Nehru these considerations counted. They were important also to ambitious junior men. To Gandhi, on the other hand, they had no personal appeal. He did not desire to join a ministry and could say little but that the leaders of Congress should decide without him.

This congressional dilemma merely widened a gap that had been growing between Gandhi and the Congress through the thirties. He did not really care about the process of organizing government or working out a constitution. Thus as the principle of Indian self-government was gradually conceded, he withdrew more and more, concentrating his attention on reforms of Hinduism or uplift of the masses by personal methods. Yet though he constantly washed his hands of what Congress was doing, the fact was that its leaders could not proceed without him. His influence on the mass of the people was so enormous that he had to be

on their side.   Congress politicians made pilgrimages to remote Sevagram, cursing the difficulties and delays, yet finding themselves when they got there as much as ever under
the spell of the man.

World War II

WHILE GANDHI WAS working quietly in Sevagram and Congress was attacking the practical problems of government, Hitler was advancing toward the Second World War in calculated steps. From the depths of his innocence at Sevagram, Gandhi was inclined to view Hitler with favorable eyes, drawing comparisons between the rise of the Indian nation and the recovery of Germany. He was not unwilling that the Germans should help destroy the British Empire, while his trust in human nature gave him no understanding of Hitler personally. He could not conceive that the dictator's heart would not be melted by the nonviolent resistance of Jews or Czechs. Gandhi's position kept drawing him into making public pronouncements that bore no relation to the actual world situation. Thus when war finally broke out, he had no positive message. He was certain that nonviolence was a higher way than war, but his intelligence had condemned the appeasement of Hitler by Neville Chamberlain. He felt no enthusiasm for either side, had no solutions, and was totally crushed by the negative aspects of war.

Since the federal constitution had never gone into effect, the central government of India was still directed by the Viceroy, who now declared that India was at war with Hitler. This was in a sense his constitutional duty, but it was only natural that Congress should be violently affronted, because no Indian group had been consulted. Unwilling to make common cause with Hitler, yet determined to resist being dragged at the heels of Britain, congressional ministries in the seven provinces resigned, leaving their governors to carry on by emergency decrees.

The fall of France in 1940 and the prospect of the imminent defeat of Great Britain aroused Gandhi to action. He wrote to the Viceroy, now Lord Linlithgow, to say that British persistence in carrying on a losing war would only result in greater bloodshed. "Hitler is not a bad man," he added hopefully. "If you call it off today, he will follow suit. If you want to send me to Germany or anywhere else, I am at your disposal. You can also inform the Cabinet about this." Lord Linlithgow was a practical man, and the times were unsuitable for this sort of fantasy. He replied that Britain would fight on and that everything would be all right.

Gandhi was unconvinced. For all his enmity toward the British, the blitz on London, which he knew so well, was unbearable to him. He published an appeal to "Every Briton" to lay down his arms. "You will invite Herr Hitler and Signor Mussolini to take what they want of the countries you call your possessions. Let them take possession of your beautiful island with its many beautiful buildings. You will give all these, but neither your minds nor your souls." While he was writing these words, Hitler was planning to deport from conquered Britain every man between seventeen and forty-five. But Gandhi had not the faintest conception of the nature of modern war.

Perhaps he knew himself that he had been driven into a dream world. At all events, his nerves were on edge. The Sevagram community had collected all sorts of peculiar people with epileptic fits or strange compulsions. Gandhi himself got into states where he fussed about trifles and upset everyone for days on end. The place, as his visitors agreed, resembled a madhouse.

At this point in the war, Gandhi was unwilling to lead a revolt and gain Indian independence at the price of British ruin. On the other hand, the principle of nonviolence forbade him to give any assistance. Congress, more politically minded, was willing, perhaps even eager to take part in fighting Hitler, but only at the price of political concessions. Lord Linlithgow, the Viceroy, responsible to the government in London that was now headed by that old imperialist Winston Churchill, was in no position to grant any real increase of liberty. Britain's back was against the wall, and the moment was not suitable for transfers of power. Thus Congress, which had actually signalized its independence of Gandhi by making overtures to the Viceroy, was soon appealing to the old man to direct a policy of resistance that neither he nor they desired to push to extremes.

Gandhi had always maintained that an absolutely perfect *Satyagrahi* could work a miracle all by himself. This seemed the moment to put his theory into practice. He selected Vinoba Bhave, his earliest Indian disciple, to travel around making antiwar speeches. Bhave did so and was arrested in three days. Nehru was chosen to follow, but was arrested before he could even begin. Lord Linlithgow was determined to keep peace in India for the duration at any price. Patel was arrested a few days later and followed to jail by about four hundred Congress leaders by the end of 1940.

India seethed with a thousand rumors, but was generally quiet.

At the end of 1941 a new phase of war was opened by the Japanese attack on Pearl Harbor. Within a month the British Far Eastern Empire was collapsing. Singapore fell in February 1942, to be followed by Rangoon in March. The Japanese were at the gates of India.

If India fell, then China must fall, for Chiang Kai-shek's lifeline of supplies would be cut off. Indeed, if India fell, it was most probable that the war would be lost by Great Britain before the power of the United States could be brought to bear. Cooperation from Indian leaders now seemed essential to England. Political prisoners had already been released, and Churchill sent out Sir Stafford Cripps to India with the offer of full-fledged dominion status.

To Gandhi, the Cripps offer was merely a blank check on a failing bank. A defeated Britain had no power to keep India subject, so that the grant of freedom had lost meaning. Besides, the Japanese as a Far Eastern people were more acceptable to Gandhi than the imperial powers of Europe. Without knowing much about Japanese ambitions, Gandhi did not imagine that Japan would attempt to conquer India. However, if India remained loyal to England, she would almost certainly become a battleground for nations who cared little for the native population. Scorched-earth policies were already being contemplated by the British as a system of defense. Finally, the Cripps plan, even if desirable, was not acceptable. It offered dominion status to a federation that the princely states and Muslim provinces need only join if they pleased. The fact was that the British could not afford to anger the princes or Muslims, from whom most of their support in the war came. No guarantee could therefore be given that India would not split into fifty states, or even more.

Summing up the position in his mind, Gandhi concluded that the only excuse for British rule in India was that she had protected the country from invaders. Since she could no longer do so, India's interest demanded that she quit the country at once, leaving Indians to deal with the Japanese by nonviolent methods. He rose to the absurd heights of send-

Sir Stafford Cripps with Gandhi after the unsuccessful conference on Britain's proposals for Indian Dominion

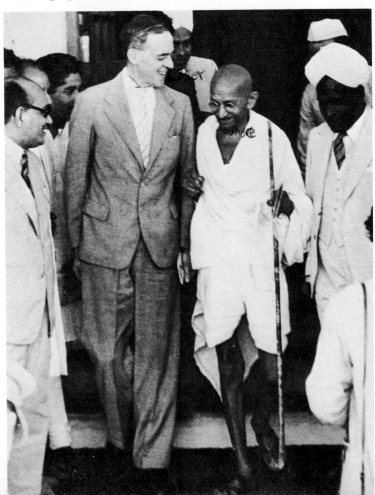

ing Mirabehn to the eastern coast, where the threat was imminent, to report on the prospects of nonviolent defense. A fantastic exchange of letters followed as Mirabehn solemnly inquired whether a *Satyagrahi* could accept British coins from Japanese or work with the invaders to restore bridges and communications in a starving countryside. Gandhi, who had no *Satyagrahis* in the area but Mirabehn herself, replied loftily that starvation was better than any form of cooperation with a conqueror. This note of unreality could only be sustained because Gandhi did not believe the Japanese would bother with India if she could only detach herself from England.

A still more important errand entrusted to Mirabehn was taking to the Working Committee of Congress a document that, Gandhi felt, could only be explained by someone who accepted his whole gospel without reservations. It was his famous "Quit India" resolution. The British must leave immediately, without stopping to make arrangements for a government to replace them. Let India go back to anarchy and solve her problems for herself. "I have not asked the British," he insisted, "to hand over India to the Congress or to the Muslims. Let them entrust India to God, or in modern parlance to anarchy. Then all the parties will fight one another like dogs, or will, when real responsibility faces them, come to a reasonable agreement. I still expect nonviolence to arise out of that chaos." Vaguely he spoke of a million lives being a small sacrifice for the independence of united India, but he never really envisaged the meaning of these terrible words. Incurably optimistic about human nature, he could not resist expecting a peaceful solution at the very moment when he was welcoming chaos.

The leading members of the Working Committee were far more practical politicians than Gandhi, but they too despaired of ever wresting from Britain independence on acceptable terms. No doubt anarchy made little appeal to them; but they thought the war was lost and saw the advantages of confusion, which they might hope to control, when the alternative was being mangled by both contesting parties. They were in a mood to support Gandhi's demand for a concession that the British could not possibly grant if they meant to go on fighting. To assist the Chinese and to build up a base in the Far East, India was more essential to the war than ever.

Once Gandhi had made up his mind to an outright breach with the British, he recovered his old fire. In August 1942, he spoke to the Congress Working Committee, giving them for a motto in the coming resistance campaign, "Do or Die!" He called in the plainest terms for "open rebellion." These were not nonviolent sayings, and Gandhi seemed unclear what he was asking for. He envisaged an Indian uprising that would tear down the present structure of the country, burying in the ruins not only the British, but the princes and dissident Muslims. Undoubtedly he thought of it as being nonviolent, but merely because in those terrible times he needed desperately to believe that nonviolence was more effective. He made no effort to penetrate the plans of a Congress group for more drastic measures. In 1922, he had called off *Satyagraha* because of the massacre at Chauri Chaura. In 1930, he had laid all blame for violence on the police for giving provocation. By 1942, he was permitting plans for violent action, even while telling himself that *Satyagraha* would prevail. In the middle of a world war, it was not easy for the prophet of *Satyagraha* to keep his head.

As a result of his own confusion, Gandhi, who had hitherto planned the strategy of his campaigns with the greatest care, now seemed uncertain what he wanted. First he spoke of a

nationwide *hartal,* adding a warning against violence. Then
he canceled the *hartal,* deciding on a massive refusal to pay
taxes. During the last decade, he had increasingly relied on
intuition, allowing an inner voice to tell him when to fast.
Perhaps he was waiting for intuition now; or maybe age and
fatigue made him impatient of detail. But he warned the
Viceroy that he meant business, sending Mirabehn to explain
to her compatriots that, "You are faced with two alternatives;
one to declare India's independence, and the other to kill
Gandhiji . . . You do not know the latent power lying buried
in this coming move. Even we do not know the force of
Gandhiji's spirit, but I can sense it, and I tell you that if the
rebellion has to burst, this viceroy will have to face a more
terrible situation than any Indian viceroy has ever had to
face before." These were strong words to a government that
had never forgotten the bloody Indian Mutiny of 1858.

Lord Linlithgow needed no further invitation to act. On
August 9, 1942, Gandhi was arrested, together with Mahadev
Desai and Mirabehn, who had just got back from her errand.
They were taken not to Yeravda Jail, but to the palace of the
Aga Khan at Poona, which had been surrounded by barbed
wire and a cordon of police. Here the prisoners were joined
by Kasturbai, and here a few days later Mahadev Desai died
of a heart attack, depriving Gandhi of the best secretary he
ever had and of a devoted adherent who knew how to handle
him in his difficult moods.

Gandhi's arrest had taken him utterly by surprise. He had
assumed that Britain, with Japan at her very door, must negotiate with him. India's situation had demanded rapid decisions of which Gandhi had been incapable because his view
of human nature, his theory of political action, and his cal-
culation of chances had all to be reviewed. He had supposed
that the Viceroy would give him time to make his plans, and

he had been wrong. The uprising of 1942, triggered off by his arrest, ran its course without his direction. It soon became clear that with his tacit permission, if not with his knowledge, violent attacks, particularly on communications, had been planned. Railway stations, post offices, and police stations were the chief targets. Police and revenue officers were murdered, and many parts of the country were cut off. In Bengal, where General Wavell was gathering strength to oppose a Japanese invasion, supply lines were severed. Troops needed for defense had to be employed to put rebellion down.

Isolated from these events in the Aga Khan's palace, Gandhi raged. He could see from the reports in the papers that the rebellion had come within measurable distance of success. It had almost managed to produce the anarchy for which he craved; and he could not fail to suppose that it might have succeeded had it not been for his untimely arrest. What made him angrier than ever was that the government, not content with putting down disorder, was laying the blame for violence on his head. His conscience was clear. He had not desired violence, and he had expected that nonviolent measures would have proved more effective in practice. Indeed, he was sure they would have done so under his direction. It was all the fault of the government, which had on the one hand deprived the movement of his leadership, while on the other it blamed the leader for the consequences.

He could not refrain from writing a series of letters to the Viceroy in defense of his honor, threatening that he might undertake a fast in protest. In response to Gandhi's requests that he be convinced if he was in error, the goaded Viceroy pointed out that Gandhi's mind was completely closed to conviction. "You have expressed profound distrust of the public reports of the recent happenings, although in your last letter on the basis of the same information, you have not hesitated to lay the whole blame for them on the government of India." He went on to demolish Gandhi's extraordinary argument that his arrest was in violation of the pact with Lord Irwin, which, as he alleged, had given him permission to make any plans for rebellion, short of violence. Linlithgow's final shot, a protest against the fast, is as well aimed as the others. "I would welcome a decision on your part to think better of it, not only because of my natural reluctance to see you willfully risk your life, but because I regard the use of a fast for political purposes as a form of political blackmail for which there can be no moral justification."

It was not often that anyone replied to Gandhi with such devastating frankness. A year later, when Linlithgow's term as viceroy came to an end, Gandhi wrote to him, saying that Linlithgow had caused him more sorrow than any other functionary of government because he had countenanced untruth about "your ex-friend." Linlithgow made answer that "as gently as I may" he must make plain that he was unable to accept Gandhi's interpretation. Gandhi had fasted in protest for twenty-one days, but it had made no difference. Far more tragic than this exchange was the reappearance of famine in India after a lapse of many years, due partly to the breakdown in communications caused by the rebellion, partly to shipping shortages and other wartime troubles, partly to the government's putting the interests of the war effort above those of the people. While each side was blaming the other, more than a million died.

None of the prisoners in the Aga Khan's palace seemed to prefer it to the familiar jail at Yeravda. They were strictly isolated and found this depressing, while the luxury of their surroundings made no appeal. But the person who suffered most was Kasturbai. She had no one to wait on, no kitchen in which to prepare the meals, no service to offer. Others read or wrote and took Gandhi's dictation; and while they did so, Kasturbai had nothing to do. Her restlessness became disturbing, and Gandhi took patiently in hand the task of giving her lessons in reading and writing. It was a long time since he had tried to teach her, and his impatience was all gone. He would sit there, showing her the provinces of India on a map or demonstrating the lines of latitude and longitude on an orange. Kasturbai did not make much progress, even though she tried. What he was telling her bore no relation to anything in her own life, so that her wandering memory could not retain it. It was becoming plain that she needed companionship on a simpler level. Gandhi's two doctors, one a disciple and the other a government appointee, both agreed. In March 1943, they won permission for her to have a great-niece, Manubehn Gandhi, as nurse-companion. Manubehn was fifteen years old and was in prison elsewhere for taking part in the "Quit India" campaign.

After the coming of Manubehn, Kasturbai was more cheerful; but in a few months her health once more declined. Her heart was bad, and she suffered from shortness of breath. Presently she could no longer sleep lying down and cradled her head on a table that was placed across her bed. She wanted to see her sons before she died. Manilal was in South Africa, but the other three were summoned to Poona and given permission to visit their mother. Harilal was turned away at the gate because he was drunk. Finally he made a visit, and Kasturbai was overjoyed; yet when she wanted to see him again, he had vanished. Eventually he was tracked down and brought to see his mother, but once more he was drunk. Poor Kasturbai suffered pains in her chest after he left. Pneumonia had set in, and Devadas wished to have her given penicillin; but Gandhi was determined to prevent it.

Kasturbai Gandhi

He knew that Ba was dying and did not wish to interfere with nature's laws.

On February 22, 1944, Kasturbai died in Gandhi's arms. They had been married sixty-two years; and he had written of her long after his vow to live with her as a sister, "She moves me as no other woman can." She was a part of himself, and he had treated her as such. A visitor to Gandhi made the comment that he seldom spoke to her and that though her eyes followed him everywhere, he hardly glanced in her direction. Yet when they were together, her place was always beside him. She retained the rare privilege of grumbling at him, and was one of the few people in his personal life who did not kiss his feet.

The prisoners gave her a Hindu funeral, performing all the necessary rites. There was even a pile of sandalwood logs in the palace, bought by the government for Gandhi's own cremation during the course of his fast against Lord Linlithgow. Her body burned all day long, so that people tried to persuade Gandhi to go to his room and lie down, for he was exhausted. "How can I leave her during her last moments on earth after we have lived for sixty-two years together?" he protested. "She would never forgive me if I did." Theirs had been one of those marriages of two incompatible people, which had meant a great deal to both, but in a fashion which outsiders could never understand. Kasturbai had suffered, yet she also had learned much by serving her husband as the ideal Hindu wife should do. For his part, Gandhi perceived this and felt his loss.

"She was an indivisible part of me," he said, "and her going has left a vacuum which will never be filled." He seemed for a while to be lost without her; and six weeks after her death, he came down with malaria. The doctors were seriously alarmed, but only with difficulty could they persuade him to take quinine. In a little over two weeks, when he was considered out of danger, the government announced that the prisoners would be released unconditionally.

Gandhi left on the hour that the guards were removed, after having asked the government if he could buy the small plots in which Kasturbai and Mahadev Desai were buried. The government answered that it was in no position to tell the Aga Khan to sell his land, but that people would be permitted to bring flowers and offer prayers. Gandhi's last imprisonment was over. It might have been imagined that his active life was over, too; but that was not the case.

The Great Opponent

MOHAMMED ALI JINNAH, the creator of Pakistan, was the son of a Muslim merchant in Karachi, though actually, like Gandhi, he descended from Gujarati stock of Kathiawar. Seven years younger than Gandhi but precociously brilliant, he arrived in London to study law in 1892 when he was only sixteen. He returned to India sophisticated, westernized in dress and manner, and with a considerable knowledge of English political life. He had learned to pay little attention to the rules of his faith, and he later took the almost unheard-of step of marrying a Parsee girl. Islam was less his religion than part of his nationality; like the color of his skin he took it for granted.

He had an excellent mind, which soon brought him to prominence as a lawyer in Bombay. While Gandhi was occupied in South Africa, Jinnah was making a name for himself in the Congress as an able negotiator of agreements between Muslim and Hindu on the governmental level. His big triumph was a pact signed at Lucknow in 1916 between

Hindu and Muslim providing that a certain number of Muslim candidates should be chosen by Muslims only for an elected General Assembly. This principle, which was conceded by the British in the Act of 1919, was considered by political Muslims to be fundamental.

In 1918, when Gandhi began to make his mark on Indian politics, Jinnah was just turned forty and established, both in the Muslim League and in the Congress as a leader of the educated Muslim group. Gandhi's pact with the instigators of the Khilafat movement was intensely distasteful to him for a number of reasons. In the first place, as a student of politics, Jinnah knew quite well that the Khilafat agitation was ridiculous in the light of the situation within the Turkish Empire. In the second place, by making this alliance, Gandhi had brought the Muslims into his camp without ever facing the problems that really divided them from Hindus and would in Jinnah's view continue to do so. Finally, Jinnah did not believe in either Gandhi or his methods.

Jinnah was essentially a worldly man with little interest in Gandhi's religious approach or his personal goodness. He regarded Gandhi's foibles with a contemptuous eye, judging them without being affected by either his charm or his character. To him, the notion of reducing India to a dependence on cottage industries was ridiculous. Similarly, to regard Hindu-Muslim unity as a simple question of changing the attitudes of individual villagers was rather like trying to substitute simple addition for a complicated problem in calculus. Jinnah felt this all the more sourly because Gandhi, despite what he thought about himself, was pure Hindu, unquestionably heir to the Hindu revivalism of Tilak. It was Gandhi who called for Congress speeches to be made in Hindustani, which he thought of as a national language. It was Gandhi who popularized homespun and the white forage cap, which lent themselves better to adaptations of Hindu costume than of Muslim. With Tilak it had been possible to negotiate, because Tilak knew where he stood as a Hindu leader. Gandhi, on the other hand, because he used bits of the Koran in prayers or had a number of Muslim friends, behaved as though he were also a super-Muslim, capable of speaking for that whole community without consulting those of its leaders who did not agree with him.

The *Satyagraha* campaign of 1920 aroused Jinnah's instant antagonism. He was still convinced that Indian affairs would make better progress by negotiation than by harnessing the power of the ignorant masses. He saw Gandhi's forces for what they were, namely an alliance of fanatical Muslims with the Hindu revival movement started by Tilak. Naturally he did not fail to observe that, though Gandhi had begun his agitation by demanding redress of the Khilafat, Rowlatt, and Amritsar wrongs, he had soon changed his tune. "*Swaraj* in a Year" had no particular Muslim appeal. In 1922, Gandhi

Mohammed
Ali Jinnah,
leader of the
Muslim League

felt himself able to discontinue his whole campaign after Chauri Chaura without giving any further thought to the Muslim cause. Jinnah drifted away from Congress and, as a result, began to consider the Muslim League as an opposition party.

The differences between Hindu and Muslim were, as Jinnah recognized, deeply rooted. The Muslims, though in a minority, had been rulers of India before the British. They still regarded themselves as being superior, encouraged by their religion, which unlike that of the Hindus, claimed to be the only true one. Despite their numerical inferiority, they wanted at least equal status. As it happened, the Hindu parts of India had been under British domination considerably longer than those parts mainly Muslim, with the consequence that Western education had gone further among Hindus. Indian civil servants, capitalists, even lawyers were largely Hindu; while the Muslim, being a latecomer to these professions, found the cards stacked against him. Gandhi, who seldom interfered with the social structure of things, showed no understanding of Muslim resentment against Hindu economic competition. Finally, the demand for independence was primarily a Hindu demand. Many a Muslim, including at times Jinnah himself, felt that the British were more likely to protect Muslim interests than Congress, in which Muslims were always a minority group.

These thoughts festered in Jinnah during the 1920s, and no overtures were made toward him by Congress. Thus, for instance, he supported the Simon Commission in 1927, accepting the fact that a parliamentary commission must be made up of members of Parliament and therefore could contain no Indians. To Jinnah the Simon Commission was an indication of British willingness to negotiate that ought to have been followed up. Partly out of disgust at the way things were going, he spent a good deal of time in Europe, returning to India only after the Nehru Committee had published its recommendations.

This was unfortunate; but in any case the Nehru Committee had made no attempt to consult the Muslim League, preferring to use the Muslims who were connected with Congress. It was not until Jinnah returned in considerable anger and published fourteen Muslim demands that the importance of Motilal Nehru's mistake could be understood. For the demands were unreasonable. They might have been a basis for negotiations before the committee report had taken shape; but as definite objections to that report, they were unacceptable. Congress might close its eyes to the Muslim League, assuring everybody that all honest patriots were inside the Congress Party; but this did not carry conviction to either the British or the Muslim world. The split was obvious.

The 1920s and 1930s were a period of rapid change inside India, by no means entirely among the Hindus. By now the ferment of national feeling had infected the Muslims, stimulating among them a fresh pride in their traditions and a reinterpretation of Muslim thought. Much of this was due to the influence of a great Muslim national poet called Iqbal. The result of it was that the Muslim League, though less in the limelight even among Muslims than the Congress Party, gained steadily in importance.

The Round Table Conference increased Jinnah's bitterness. How far his importance had declined since 1916 may be seen by the fact that the British did not appoint him as head of the Muslim delegation. They chose the Aga Khan, indeed a powerful potentate, but a man who lived very little in India, preferring Paris, the Riviera, and his racing stable in England to the society of his fellow Muslims. To Jinnah, a man of great personal ambition who was never happy playing second fiddle, this was an intolerable slight.

Soured by his position in the conference, Jinnah was in no mood to be charmed by Gandhi, who showed himself at this time sublimely unconscious of other points of view. We have seen how he opposed the separate electorates for untouchables that were desired by Dr. Ambedkar. He was antagonistic to separate electorates for Muslims, and for the same reason. They would, he said, perpetuate the differences between Muslim and Hindu. In this, Gandhi was perfectly right; but his position was illogical because he did not wish to merge Muslim and Hindu in a common religion or common social customs. Thus the differences were bound to remain, and they therefore required political expression. Though eventually he gave in, Gandhi persisted in his opposition to separate Muslim electorates long enough to convince Jinnah that Congress was anxious to repudiate the agreement of 1916.

The failure of the Round Table Conference was not, in Jinnah's opinion, primarily the fault of the British. So disgusted was he with the Indians themselves that he thought seriously of establishing himself in England. His wife was dead, and he had disowned his daughter for marrying a non-Muslim after his own example. He felt intensely lonely and seems to have imagined that he might carve out a distinguished legal career for himself in London or enter Parliament, where he could represent Indian interests. He had not the luck, however, and perhaps the ease with people that had distinguished Dadabhai Naoroji. Early in 1935 he returned to India.

The new Government of India Act, which became law in 1935, led to elections for the eleven provinces under British rule, shortly after Jinnah's return. The elections found the

Muslims split between Congress Party and Muslim League. If both were to put up candidates for every possible seat, it followed that the Muslim vote would be divided. Perceiving the difficulty, the Muslim League approached Congress with the suggestion that, in provinces with a large Muslim minority, a coalition ministry should be formed with a certain proportion of the new ministers belonging to the Muslim League. If this were understood, the League would refrain from opposing Congress Muslims.

Congress was willing to negotiate, for on the eve of the election it had lost Gandhi's sublime confidence that it represented eighty-five percent of the people. But when the election returns showed a Congress landslide in seven of the provinces, Congress pointed out that a party only entered coalitions if it had not got a majority without one. Thus all-Congress ministries were established in seven provinces, and the Muslim League found itself outside in the cold. What made matters worse was the assurance that they always would be outside because Muslims were in a minority in these provinces. Nor did Congress Muslims find themselves much better off. They had all the apparatus of a party, but nowhere to go, small chance of ever rising to the top.

Jinnah had quit India in despair. He returned in a cold rage. In 1935, Hitler was well established in power, and his success was extremely interesting to all the have-nots in politics, including Jinnah. He admired the ease with which Hitler used a sense of grievance to knit his people together, as well as the effectiveness of his determined show of brute force. It had by now occurred to Jinnah that there were other solutions for the Indian Muslim than always being a minority group in Hindu India. Hitler talked about Pan-Germanism and claimed allegiance from Germans scattered all over the world. Muslims belonged to a vast community stretching from the borders of China to Istanbul, Egypt, and Morocco. A suggestion had already been made that north-west India should combine with Iran, Afghanistan, and neighboring areas to form a state entitled Pakistan, or "Land of the Pure," the title being composed, more or less, out of the initials of five Indian provinces and three neighboring ones. Jinnah saw possibilities in the scheme and the title, for though there was little prospect of Afghanistan's or Iran's adhering to it, Pakistan provided a rallying cry for Muslim India.

It is difficult to be sure when Jinnah first decided to set himself up as an imitation Hitler and when he made up his mind to partition India. The two dates are not the same, for there was a period in which he was inclined to use the increasing power of the Muslim League to force concessions out of Congress. Clearly by the time that the Congress ministries were established in the provinces, Jinnah had lost all confidence in his power to cooperate with them. By 1940, he saw like everyone else that Britain's rule in India was doomed and that the only task that remained was to decide on Britain's successor. Gandhi, when he called on the British to quit India in 1942, thought he was proposing that the country should return to anarchy. Though he foresaw that there might be fighting "like dogs," he was optimistic that the crisis would produce a peaceful solution. But Gandhi stood for a united India and assumed that every patriot did the same. Jinnah, who also foresaw that things might come to a fight, set about preparing to win it.

The technique of his organization was surprisingly like Hitler's, adapted to Muslim beliefs and Indian conditions. It was not until the forties that Jinnah took the title of Quaid-e-Azam, or "Great Leader," but he used many of Hitler's methods to consolidate his party. To wealthy Muslims he offered ancient Muslim glory as described by the poet Iqbal. To ambitious ones, he offered a chance of political office in a country ruled for Muslims and by Muslims. He manipulated the Muslim priesthood and the fanatic rank and file by playing on hatred. Deliberately the Muslim League recruited members, as the Congress had done during the previous decade. It organized them in local groups, ostensibly to teach them pride in their Muslim heritage, but actually to foster their hate of their Hindu neighbors, broadcasting among them newspapers and pamphlets full of stories of Hindu ill treatment. Next the Muslim League moved to isolate Congress Muslims by claiming on every occasion to represent all Muslims. These tactics converted many Congress politicians who saw themselves being left high and dry, individuals lost in Congress without the support of a real Muslim party.

It is only fair to assume that Jinnah was a patriot in his way, just as Gandhi was in his. But Jinnah was personally a friendless man who has left few people to defend his character. Admirers of Gandhi thought Jinnah a compound of ambition, vanity and vindictiveness, adding that he tore India apart in order to play the great man among his fellow Muslims. They consider this all the more inexcusable because Jinnah had tuberculosis and was in 1946 a dying man. For the sake of a short hour of glory to which he left no heir, Jinnah, as they point out, provoked the massacre or displacement of fifteen million people. However, though there is no doubt that Jinnah did have these evil qualities and that he manipulated fanaticism without being a fanatic himself, we have to give him credit for an acute political mind, much worldly wisdom, a realistic approach to facts, and a genuine understanding of the position of Indian Muslims. He did indeed foresee that there would be no place for a Muslim

"Great Leader" in a united India, but he had not taken the title until he felt he had exhausted his chances of reaching an agreement with Congress.

The British are also blamed for the partition of India on the grounds that they were in a position to force both princes and Muslims to give way to the Congress Party. Undoubtedly this was the case at the Round Table Conference and later in the thirties. An agreement could have been reached at that time if the British had imposed it. It was, however, hardly fair to ask them to sacrifice minorities that had been persistently faithful to them. They did in the end sacrifice the princes, and have been accused of bad faith for doing so. But the Muslims, the Sikhs, the untouchables, and other minority groups also looked to Britain for protection.

In 1944, when Gandhi was released after the death of Kasturbai, it had become obvious that the war would be won by the allies. A Japanese invasion was no longer a menace, which meant that another campaign against the British could do little for India and would make Congress unpopular with the winning side. Nevertheless, for consistency's sake, Gandhi needed to raise the question of India's freedom. After going to jail in 1942 with a "Quit India" slogan on his lips and a motto of "Do or Die!" he could hardly come out in 1944 and say nothing. Accordingly, as soon as he had recovered his health, he demanded that popular government should be restored in the provinces and that a central Indian government should be set up. The Viceroy, Lord Wavell, replied that there could be no question of Indian independence before the end of the war, but that he would accept a transitional government along the lines of the 1935 act, provided that it was composed of Hindus, Muslims, and other important minorities. In effect, therefore, unless Hindus and Muslims could come to agreement, the government would have to go on as it was until the end of the war.

There was nothing that Gandhi could do but talk with Jinnah in hopes of working out a compromise between them. It was too late. Jinnah was too astute to refuse an interview; but since he really wanted partition, he had no intention of coming to an agreement. It was easy for him to raise objections. Gandhi, for instance, had come to him as an individual, hoping to work out a formula that he could persuade Congress to ratify. Jinnah pointed out that he himself represented the Muslims, and Gandhi obviously represented the Hindus. If he did not, there was no point in talking any further. Much of the conversation went along these lines, Gandhi determined not to be backed into the position of admitting that Congress was pure Hindu, while Jinnah insisted that the Muslim League be recognized as representative of a Muslim Indian "nation" with its own separate civilization, laws, customs, traditions, and hopes for the future. This was not the kind of negotiation Gandhi was used to, for in general it was he who made the demands. Nor could he make his usual personal impression on a man who knew him well and had never liked him. The conversations went on for several days, tailing off into silences that were only broken because the little man who must have things his way could not accept defeat on an issue so close to his heart. Eventually he had to face it, however, for he had no means of putting pressure upon Jinnah. To this situation, nonviolent resistance could not apply. He considered fasting, but dismissed the idea. It would not have affected Jinnah's resolution, while he yet might need his strength and health to battle, quite how he did not know, for a united India.

The talks came to an end without any agreement. Gandhi

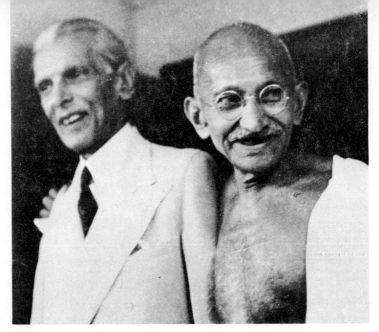
Gandhi meets with Mohammed Ali Jinnah to discuss the Hindu-Muslim conflict

departed for Sevagram, where he tried to recover from his failure by observing a vow of silence and meditating sadly over his own and India's problems. Jinnah, on the other hand, when asked by the press if there would be further meetings, replied acidly: "Mr. Gandhi says that it depends on his inner voice. I have no admission to that place. I cannot say."

For over six months the deadlock continued. The crisis could not be put off indefinitely because the war was coming to an end. The Indian army of two and a quarter million men would need to be brought home and to a large extent disbanded, with consequences nobody could foresee. In June 1945, Lord Wavell thought it time to summon a meeting of Congress and Muslim leaders to talk the situation over. Jinnah promptly demanded that the Muslims, who were about a quarter of the total Indian population, should have equal representation with the Hindus. Such a demand could not be acceptable to Congress, which, however, offered no constructive alternative plan. Gandhi, discouraged by the failure of his previous effort with Jinnah, would only attend as a private citizen and made no contribution.

Leaving the conference in despair, Gandhi retired to a nature clinic outside Poona for treatments and decided that he ought to reorganize the clinic to make it a spot where the poor could be treated on the same terms as the rich. For months he busied himself with this project, only to throw it up in the end and retire to a small village, where he set himself up as a doctor, prescribing sunbaths, fruit juices, and the recitation of the name of God.

He was hiding his head in the sand, fearing to look at the future; but Congress needed him still and was persistent. India's situation was becoming more dangerous than ever. The Royal Indian Navy mutinied in February 1946. Riots were spreading in Bombay, Calcutta and Madras. The British could not keep the peace in India much longer, whether they wanted to or not. Besides, the new Labour government of Great Britain was actually anxious to let India go and turn its attention to social reform. Prime Minister Attlee sent over three Cabinet members with authority to discuss the future of India and make decisions. Two of them were long-time personal friends and admirers of Gandhi. In other words, Gandhi himself might wish to retire into private life, but the British would not let him, rightly sensing that without him there could be no accord with India.

He came to Delhi and established himself in a hut in the slums, to which the British mission and the Congress leaders resorted. The British attempted to find a formula for a united India that would satisfy Jinnah, who assented, only to find objections later. Congress, in its own way as unreasonable as Jinnah, perceived that an interim government would have to be formed somehow, and was tempted by the prospect of forming it alone without any agreement with the Muslim League. Gandhi, suspicious of the Viceroy, merely repeated the suggestion that the British withdraw and allow Indians to settle their own affairs.

This was just what Jinnah proposed to do. In the middle of August he, too, announced that Indians would settle the issues. For some time he had been talking about "Direct Action" in case of failure of negotiations. Now he designated August 16 as Direct Action Day. At this signal, the Muslims of the Calcutta slums turned on their Hindu neighbors.

The move had been well planned in advance and was executed by the *goondas* or hooligans of the Calcutta slums which, swollen by industrial expansion due to the war, were among the worst in the world. For four days Calcutta was out of control, during which time five thousand people were killed and many times that number were robbed, beaten, and mutilated. Whole quarters had been laid waste, and terrified refugees, herded into helpless crowds, were clamoring for protection.

A horrified hush fell over India. Muslims and Hindus were so inextricably mixed that there could be no telling where the next storm would burst. Lord Wavell's anxiety inclined him to bring pressure on Congress in favor of Jinnah, who had again hinted that he might after all enter a coalition. Wavell's well-meant efforts merely caused Congress to look on him as their enemy and secretly anxious to put Jinnah in control. Thus the more earnestly the British government tried to disengage itself from India, the more the two factions devoted their energies to a naked struggle for power.

Walk Alone

Two months after the riots in Calcutta, terror broke out in Noakhali, a water-logged region lying between the Ganges and Brahmaputra rivers, highly fertile and densely populated. Here once again the Muslims turned on the Hindus, gangs of murderers spreading the plague by traveling from village to village. Men were cut down, women raped and mutilated, children hacked to pieces, corpses thrown into public wells. So terrible were the massacres and so cut off was the district that the murders had been going on for a full week before news of it seeped out to the rest of India.

Ever since his release from jail, now two years earlier, Gandhi had been at a loss. He had tried to disentangle himself from events that were out of his control, but he had been too long in command to abdicate. He had vacillated, moving unhappily from discussions with Jinnah to doctoring the poor and back to conferences with leaders of Congress who cared about issues to which he was indifferent. Nothing had gone as he desired, and it seemed possible that he would see his lifework destroyed before his eyes. He was seventy-seven. At last, however, when the news came in from Noakhali, Gandhi knew what he had to do. He would go to Noakhali in person to reestablish peace. He did not know how he would do this and did not speak Bengali, which was the language of the people there. His life, for what it was worth, would certainly be in danger, both from Muslims and maddened Hindus. The rise of the militant Muslim League had given impetus to a parallel Hindu organization called the Hindu Mahasabha, which was by no means inclined to suffer injuries without taking vengeance. None of these considerations mattered to Gandhi. The one and only important thing was to stamp out the plague before it spread all over India.

He arrived at Noakhali and established himself in a village called Srirampur, attended only by a secretary and an interpreter. Some of his dedicated followers, including Mirabehn, had asked to come with him. He placed them in other villages, instructing them to keep the peace if necessary by offering their own lives to protect their villagers. Meanwhile, in Srirampur he talked to people, saying to women who had seen their husbands murdered before their eyes, "I have not come to bring you consolation. I have come to bring you courage." In the same tone he spoke to refugees, telling them to go back to their homes. Never inquiring which Muslims had done the hideous deeds, he insisted that they treat their fellow men like brothers for the future.

His influence had a certain effect, but he felt that it was not enough. After a few weeks his grandniece Manubehn, now eighteen years of age, had come to wait on him. He treated her as he had treated Mirabehn in London, demanding much, yet giving affection and confidence in return. He had decided to make a pilgrimage through Noakhali, which was a district so intersected by creeks and drainage

ditches that often even bullock carts could not get about.
He was going to walk, barefoot, from village to village. In
preparation, he was already practicing crossing the swaying
footbridges that linked each place with its neighbor.

He set out early in January with a bamboo staff in one
hand and often leaning with the other on Manubehn's
shoulder. His interpreter followed him and at times one or
two others joined him. They carried bundles and the spinning wheel. Behind them straggled an increasing number
of reporters. It was a scene reminiscent of the famous salt
march, save that the hero of the former occasion had moved
at a brisk pace, knowing precisely what he went to do. Now
the old man made his painful progress of five or six miles a
day from village to village along winding paths overhung by
tropical vegetation. Often he was not made welcome.
People were surly either because of bad conscience or because they were frightened of the gangs of bullies still known
to be around. Once he met fresh excrement in his path and
stooped to remove it with the aid of leaves in full view of
villagers who knew no deeper degradation for a Hindu.
Mildly he remarked that they ought to keep their paths clean
and that if they were dirtied tomorrow, he would clean them
again. Next morning there was more dirt, but the outraged
Manubehn, who had gone out early to clean it up, found a
group of villagers volunteering to help her.

Gandhi used to start about seven-thirty in the morning and
liked to sing a song of Rabindranath Tagore's as he did so:

> *Walk alone.*
> *If they answer not thy call, walk alone;*
> *If they are afraid and cower mutely facing the wall,*
> *O thou of evil luck,*
> *Open thy mouth and speak out alone.*

When he reached the next village, he would rest. The news of his appearance soon got about, attracting many from villages that did not lie in his path. He would hold a prayer meeting and talk to the people, telling them to keep themselves clean, to have peace in their hearts toward their fellows. He would send Manubehn to talk to the Muslim women, since they did not come out to see him. He himself listened to complaints, gave advice, did his spinning, and answered the letters that still reached him in this remote spot. At ten o'clock he would sleep in the house of a villager with Manubehn near him and the reporters camping as they could in tents outside. Since it was wintertime, there was much rain.

Manubehn did the cooking, washed Gandhi's feet, dressed the cuts she found there, took dictation, and packed up for the next move. On one occasion she was five minutes late in being ready, because Gandhi had gone to sleep over his papers so that she could not get at them to pack them. He was still capable of nervous states and accused her of stealing five minutes from five hundred people who were waiting to see him. It was her duty to have waked him up. Another time she left behind a special stone that was used to scrape dirt off his feet and legs. He was violently upset and sent her back for it through winding overgrown paths and in an area where the Muslims were unfriendly. The terrified girl got back with the stone almost in hysterics. "If some ruffian had carried you off," Gandhi said, "and you had met your death courageously, my heart would have danced with joy."

It was a strange incident born of the fact that Gandhi's nerves were fretted almost to breaking point. Everywhere he heard the same horrible stories, saw burnt-out houses or the blood of the slaughter still visible. He was without fear for his own life, but he could not shake off dread for

Manubehn. He knew what might happen to her after the crowd had finished with him, so that he had to put her under the protection of God before he could feel better. Everything was distorted by the horrors of Noakhali.

In October, the Hindus of Bihar had risen against their Muslim neighbors, and the same scenes of massacre were repeated. Gandhi had always been especially popular in Bihar, for in this province lay Champaran, the district in which he had first become champion of the poor. Recalled, therefore, from Noakhali by an urgent message announcing further trouble, he went in February to the provincial capital of Patna, whence he undertook a tour of villages, accompanied by a gigantic Muslim friend and admirer, Abdul Gaffar Khan, known as "the frontier Gandhi."

Meanwhile, the British government in London, perceiving that Lord Wavell could make no progress with Indian factions, sent out Lord Louis Mountbatten as viceroy in February 1947, with instructions that India was to become independent in June 1948, later emended to August 1947. There was no time to be lost, and Mountbatten wired immediately to Gandhi to come to Delhi.

He went, but the discussions were bitter to him because Mountbatten was prepared to force partition. If the Indian factions would not agree, they must disagree. Terms were offered to Jinnah and accepted, though with reluctance, because Pakistan, deprived of the Hindu sections of the Punjab and Bengal, was far less than he wanted. Congress gave consent also because no alternative to partition remained except civil war. To Gandhi, the arrangement was a disaster that made mockery of all he had tried to do for India, yet even he told people to support Congress. The decision was taken at last, but details remained to be settled.

There were so many of these that it would be impossible

to list them all. British India had been one land for a long time, and the process of dislocation could not be easy. Pakistan was bound to center in the northwest, but the Muslim section of Bengal would be separated from it by eight hundred miles of Indian territory. Among the princes, who had now to decide for one or the other, there were Muslim rulers of Hindu people, Hindu rulers of Muslims. There were areas where the balance between the two was very even. The Indian army would have to be divided with all its depots and supplies. Meanwhile, its senior officers were mostly British, as were also about fifty percent of the senior civil servants and police. It was part of Mountbatten's job to get these people with their wives and families out of India; and yet as they left, all services were thrown into temporary confusion. The more the forces of law and order were weakened, the more it was necessary to hurry the departure of Europeans who might, in the excitement of Independence Day, be massacred.

Everybody foresaw a fearful breakdown, but nobody had more than part of his time to think of it. The English were busy rescuing their people. Jinnah, whose Pakistan, broken into two parts, contained almost nothing of India's industrial wealth, no middle class that was not Hindu, and no port worth the name except Karachi, was busy trying to take in territory by extravagant promises to the neighboring princes. Congress, though equally determined to get the lion's share of the princely states, had another problem on its mind that paralyzed its activities. The going of the British had left an enormous number of jobs to be filled. Every leading party member, even if assured of a position of great power, had always hosts of needy cousins to provide for and Congress hangers-on. The struggle for the spoils was naked and shameful, sickening Gandhi to the very soul. It was natural because the economic discontent of the educated classes had caused them to turn to Congress in the first place. But it did not befit the servants of India, as Gandhi liked to think of politicians.

Through the efforts of Mountbatten, one concession to the need of the times was extorted from Jinnah. He consented to put his name beside that of Gandhi on a proclamation deploring acts of violence and denouncing the use of force for political ends. It called on the people to refrain not only from violent acts, but from provocative words in speech or writing. This proclamation, however, was meaningless because the situation was one that called for drastic preventative action, not for words. In the Punjab, the Sikhs, a small minority of a few millions, many of whom had been incorporated against their will in Pakistan, were sharpening swords. In Kashmir, the Hindu ruler of a largely Muslim population wanted to adhere to India and had arrested the leader of the Muslim agitation. In Bihar and Noakhali there were fresh riots.

There was nothing for Gandhi to do in Delhi, where the intrigues of Congress members sickened him. He went back to Bihar and then on to Kashmir, taking with him two grand-nieces, Manubehn and Abhabehn, who were to be with him from this time to the end. But in Kashmir, he could make little impression. Everybody seemed to have gone insane. He thought that he ought to go back to Noakhali and finish his interrupted tour, but he did so by way of Patna and Calcutta.

In Calcutta the city fathers met him, begging him to remain. Independence Day was approaching, and this would mean the severance of East from West Bengal. There were the usual difficulties, economic and social, involved in the partition. Calcutta, in which all these tensions were con-

centrated, was like a city doused in gasoline and waiting for
the first firecracker of Independence Day to set it off. The
enormous city had never been quiet since the tragic riots
of the preceding year. Law and order had very nearly broken
down, and the *goondas* openly terrorized whole districts.
It was thought that the Hindus were planning to rise and
take bloody revenge for the great massacre. Muslim officials
and people who could afford to move had already fled to
East Bengal, but poorer Muslims clung to shops and liveli-
hoods in Calcutta. At their wits' end, the worthies of the
city told Gandhi that he alone could prevent a civil war.

Gandhi was reluctant to stay, for he felt that he was committed to Noakhali; but he could not refuse to grant a few
days to the problems of Calcutta, provided that the Muslims
in the city would telegraph to people with whom they had
connections in Noakhali, imploring them to keep the peace.
They did so, and also sent an urgent summons to Shaheed
Suhrawardy, their leading Muslim politician, who was in
Karachi helping to form a government for Pakistan.

Shaheed Suhrawardy, who flew back to Calcutta with his
daughter, was a tough, unscrupulous politician who was
generally believed to have been the organizer behind the
massacres of Direct Action Day. He was an important member of the Muslim League, a heavy man with an overbearing
manner. Naturally he was marked down for special hatred
by the Hindus who were, especially with the approach of
partition, superior in numbers to the Muslims in the city.
Now that the tables were turned and Muslims were threatened, Suhrawardy proved that he had the qualities of a true
leader.

Gandhi, who was not disposed to inquire into the past,
rather liked Suhrawardy for his bluff directness and his
genuine concern about his people. He told Suhrawardy that

he would stay in Calcutta if the Muslim leader would join
him in some hut in the slums and go everywhere with him so
that they could show themselves to Muslim and Hindu together. Recognizing that this move would be more dangerous to Suhrawardy than to himself, he suggested that the
politician consult his daughter and decide within twenty-
four hours.

Suhrawardy rose to the occasion, and the two took up their
quarters in a largish but decrepit house on the edge of a
slimy canal that separated a Hindu slum from what had been
a Muslim area until recently, when *goondas* armed with
homemade grenades and sten guns had cleaned it out.

Gandhi moved in on August 13, two days before Independence Day, to be greeted by a crowd of belligerent Hindu
youths gathered in the filthy little yard that surrounded the
house, cursing him because he had not come when Hindus
were in trouble, but only now when the tables were turned
on the Muslims. They let him pass and even at his insistence
admitted Suhrawardy; but their numbers increased toward
evening, and soon they were stoning the windows. When
these were completely smashed, some of the youths tried to
climb into the house.

Gandhi admitted a deputation that was too angry and
excited for a time to listen to reason. Presently, however, his
calm determination had its effect. They could kill him, he
told them; but they could not prevent him from working for
peace as long as he was alive. He would not call in the
military or ask to be spared, but force would not deter him.
Presently the young men grew quieter. Some of them even
offered to keep guard over the house during the night, while
one was heard to mutter to another: "God knows, the old
man is a wizard — everyone is won over by him."

That night the crisis passed. Gandhi and his party were

able to settle themselves in three rooms that had been hastily swept out and so thoroughly dusted with insect powder that the stench was sickening. There was only one latrine, which had to do for those who were staying in the house as well as for a constant procession of Gandhi's visitors.

Next morning Gandhi held a prayer meeting in the yard, speaking solemnly of Independence Day, which was on the morrow, and arguing that freedom was meaningless unless it brought peace. The two communities must learn to live together. His words were heard with mutterings by a crowd of protesters who had gathered in equal numbers with those who came for the blessing of the saint. Presently they began to shriek for their enemy, Suhrawardy.

Gandhi had retired into the house; but at this he threw open the shutters that had been closed to protect the broken windows, summoning Suhrawardy to stand beside him. There was a great outcry as people kept asking Suhrawardy if he were responsible for the massacre. When they would not accept his answer that all were responsible, he finally shouted out boldly, "Yes, it was my responsibility!" The daring admission pleased the crowd, which actually cheered him.

Before arriving in the slum quarter, Gandhi had arranged a demonstration of Hindus and Muslims to march through the city together. About five thousand of each joined in and made a great impression, so that when the dreaded Independence Day dawned, many people were chanting in the streets, "Hindus and Muslims are brothers!"

There were grand illuminations on the Independence Day; the new national flag was everywhere; so many people flocked to the little house to see Gandhi that he had to come to the door about every half hour to give his blessing. Eventually Suhrawardy drove out with him through the re-

joicing crowds who hailed him as the Father of the Nation.
Congratulatory telegrams poured in, but Gandhi felt no
pleasure at the triumph of so many hopes and efforts. He was
oppressed by care and thought in terms of prayer or penance.

He stayed on in Calcutta because he did not dare to leave.
In the Punjab civil war had broken out, and the armed forces
of the new nation were unable to restore order. In Calcutta
there was no one capable of keeping the peace except
Gandhi. He showed himself everywhere with Suhrawardy,
going through all the motions that the situation seemed to
demand; but his heart was not in it. Once again he was
irresolute, wondering if he ought to go to the Punjab, the
sundered halves of which were filled with pitiful refugees
fleeing for their lives. Whole trains of refugees were derailed
and every traveler massacred. Many vanished and were
never heard of again. Into Pakistan or into India flowed the
dispossessed in their millions, each with his horrible tale to
tell, with his anger or despair. But Gandhi could not be there
and also in Calcutta.

About two weeks after Independence Day, a band of the
militant Hindu Mahasabha gathered outside Gandhi's house,
bringing with them a heavily bandaged man who, they said,
had been stabbed by a Muslim. Later it was discovered that
he had merely fallen off a trolley car. It happened that
Gandhi, with his two great-nieces and two servants, was all
alone in the house. Suhrawardy was not there. The young
men forced their way in, to be met by the two girls.
Abhabehn, who spoke Bengali, told them that Gandhi was
sleeping in the inner room and was in any case observing his
day of silence. They retreated as far as the yard, where they
continued yelling that Suhrawardy and his friends be surrendered to them. By this time Gandhi himself was awake,
while various people had slipped into the house to try to

protect him. It was indeed his day of silence, but he always allowed himself to break this in a crisis. He went therefore to the door, putting his hands together in the traditional Hindu greeting. He was met with such shouting and yelling that he seems to have thought his last hour had come and was only held back by his nieces from rushing out into the crowd. Someone tried to hit him with a *lathi,* while someone else threw a brick. Gandhi went back inside just as the police came up with tear gas.

Next day the Hindu Mahasabha staged a succession of riots. Bomb explosions and machine guns could be heard everywhere. Some frightened Muslims took refuge with Gandhi and asked to be evacuated from the area. A Hindu truck driver volunteered to take them to a Muslim quarter and set off; but about a hundred and fifty yards down the road, hand grenades were lobbed into the truck from a roof, killing two Muslim workmen. Gandhi, who had not seen this happen but had heard the explosion, came down the street with his interpreter and saw the two dead bodies lying in the road with the mother of one of them sitting wailing beside them, her clothes all stained with the blood of her son. Gandhi looked at her in silence, and finally he said to his interpreter: "Tell her that God gave her a son in His pleasure, and in His pleasure He has taken the son away."

"I cannot tell her that," the interpreter protested.

Some yards down the road, a crowd of Hindu youths had gathered to watch. They told the interpreter that they would protect the remaining Muslims and take them to a place of safety. They would fight their own comrades with guns and bombs to do so, for they did not understand nonviolence. But if they were arrested, Gandhi must set them free.

Gandhi had gone back to the house when the interpreter found him and passed on this request. To his astonishment,

Gandhi immediately said, "Go and tell them I am with them."

"What about nonviolence?" asked the interpreter, astonished, but Gandhi insisted. The interpreter went and met the police, who told him that everything was now in hand. He returned, therefore, to Gandhi, still puzzled, and asked him: "Why don't you tell them that violence is wrong?"

Gandhi and his companions are sobered as they view the destruction in Calcutta

"How can I say that unless I demonstrate that nonviolence is more effective? I cannot tell them that violence is wrong while I cannot give them a substitute." He looked old and tired and seemed to be coming to some desperate resolution. Someone asked him if he was thinking of a fast, and he admitted that he was praying within himself over the question.

For a fast to have its effect Gandhi needed publicity, and he sent his interpreter to summon the new Indian governor of Bengal, who was an old and tried partisan of Gandhi's in Congress. In vain did the Governor try to dissuade him. His mind was made up. Independence was only two weeks old, and India was breaking up into anarchy. If order could not be restored, then Pakistan or Britain might seize a chance to dominate, and freedom might be lost. In face of this danger, the life of one old man was of little value.

The Governor left with a form of proclamation in which Gandhi explained his reasons for a fast, which he would continue until the people of Calcutta reached an agreement to ensure peace for the future. Fairly soon important leaders were hurrying to the house in the slums to reason with Gandhi or to talk over what was to be done. The rioting throughout the city continued, and various people who went out in groups of Hindus and Muslims together to pacify the mobs were beaten or slaughtered. Nevertheless, more and more people kept coming to consult with the little man lying on his bed. Muslims had begun wondering if they would not all have their throats cut if Gandhi died fasting for their sakes. Hindu students, lawyers, even the leaders of the Hindu Mahasabha felt they could not bear the guilt which would be laid on them if they permitted Gandhi to perish. Thus numbers of people of every sort joined the fearless Suhrawardy in walking up to their enemies with expressions of peace. By the fourth day, when the fury was dying down,

a deputation of the *goondas* came to kneel beside Gandhi's
bed and surrender their weapons, promising never again to
loot or murder.

Gandhi was half-convinced that the peace could be kept,
but he would not break his fast until he was certain. People
tried to persuade him that all would be well with Calcutta,
that he could leave and go to help the Punjab. He demanded
guarantees; and finally the officials of various civic organizations signed a paper promising to keep Calcutta at peace at
the cost of their lives. Then the tough old Suhrawardy
handed Gandhi a glass of lemon juice to break his fast,
kneeling at his feet with tears in his eyes.

Delhi

As soon as he was well enough, Gandhi turned his back on Calcutta and set off for Delhi with the intention of making his way to the Punjab; but the troubles that had begun in that divided province had by now overflowed. Gandhi was greeted by a guard of soldiers on the Delhi platform, more soldiers in the streets, and universal ruin. Nobody had dared to tell him of the insane riots that had littered every street in Delhi with the dead, plundered every mosque in the town and burned the Muslim quarter. Fifteen million people were migrating, and those escaping from Pakistan had brought with them horrible tales to arouse the spirit of vengeance. *Goondas* still reigned in some of the narrow alleys of Delhi, but in the center of the city a dead hush hung over everything. A curfew had been imposed that was only lifted for four hours every day, during which frightened people hurried out to buy supplies. Hospitals were jammed with the wounded, and dead men lay unburied for lack of anyone to deal with them. Cholera and smallpox had broken out.

Gandhi had wanted to go to his old house in the slum

quarter, but this was impossible. The city was jammed as never before. Refugees were camped in the shells of burned houses, in the open courtyards of the great mosques, in the very streets. They poured in without food, without bedding, sick, wounded, and in rags. Sanitation had completely broken down, and supplies of every kind were giving out.

Lord Mountbatten, now governor-general, had taken charge of an emergency committee and was working frantically with Prime Minister Nehru and Patel to bring order out of chaos; but the task was beyond them all. Kathiawar was aflame. Kashmir was in confusion. Pakistan, which was in its turn receiving a terrible flood of fugitives from India, was threatening war. No one was in any condition to see that Pakistan, being smaller and poorer than India, was in worse confusion. Though freedom was not yet a month old, India seemed to be breaking up into chaos.

There could be no question of going on to the Punjab. Patel, who had come down to the station to meet Gandhi, took him to the house of the millionaire, G. D. Birla, which, being as big as a palace and privately owned, had room for him. They installed him in a few rooms in one corner overlooking a terraced garden.

Gandhi settled down to do what he could. He sent for Suhrawardy to keep him in touch with Jinnah and the Government of Pakistan. But Jinnah, so arrogant and decisive in negotiations, was overwhelmed by the box of troubles he had opened. He seemed unable to make up his mind and suspected friend and foe alike, drifting, sick and helpless, on the tide. Meanwhile in Delhi Gandhi became a sheltering rock in time of trouble for all the bewildered men who had scrambled into office with such alacrity a few weeks earlier. They needed his advice, his firm grip on fundamentals, his influence with the crowds, his warmth of interest and understanding. At Birla House, Gandhi's telephone was incessantly ringing. His secretaries ran messages all over Delhi; ministers came to see him in person, fitting their problems into the ordered pattern of his day, which was still imposed on that chaos by his iron will.

All around Delhi, there were camps of Muslim refugees where terrified people were waiting for transport to Pakistan. The worst of these was at a fort called Purana Qila, where seventy-five thousand were living in horrible conditions that were degenerating into utter disorder. Distribution of supplies had broken down, and it was known that large quantities of weapons and ammunition were being smuggled in. In the confusion, the Emergency Committee could not even find a loud-speaker with which they might try to control the disorganized crowd. Patel, who as minister of the interior was responsible for order, was hesitating about whether he had not better order soldiers to take the fort by storm before its inhabitants burst out in murderous frenzy.

Gandhi drove out to the fort with his two nieces and Dr. Sushila Nayyar, daughter of a friend, who had long been his personal physician. He was immediately surrounded by a shrieking mob, so that the chauffeur in panic tried to drive away again. Gandhi ordered him to stop and got out. He walked into the crowd and began to tell the people that Hindus and Muslims were alike children of God. He was still weak from his fast in Calcutta, however, and spoke in a hoarse whisper, so that one of the girls had to repeat what he said. Those listening to him were people who had lost all they possessed and suffered terribly at Hindu hands. Some of them made menacing gestures, while here and there a cry was raised of "Death to Gandhi!"

Gradually he got those nearest him to sit down and listen, and then in his turn he listened to them while they recited

Gandhi among the Muslim refugees waiting for transportation to Pakistan at the fort Purana Qila in Delhi

their complaints. While he promised to do what he could, they escorted him peacefully back to his automobile.

There were other camps and many other such scenes. In private he argued with Patel, who had made up his mind that Muslims were traitors to India who would all rise up if it came to war with Pakistan. Gandhi insisted that if Muslims were properly treated, they would be loyal to the lands of their birth. When he heard that mosques had been sacked or converted to temples, he said that they should be restored. Homes and property abandoned by terrified Muslims should be kept in custody for them, not taken as loot.

He visited Hindu refugee camps also, set up in a hurry to take care of the fugitives from Pakistan. Here too he heard the cry "Death to Gandhi!" as he preached peace to people maddened by terrible sufferings at Muslim hands. He was holding regular prayer meetings in the garden at Birla House which were broadcast by the All-India Radio. In these he was careful to include verses from the Koran, to the further indignation of Hindu extremists.

His seventy-eighth birthday came and went with congratulations from all over the world and ceremonial visits from everyone who was of importance in Delhi. He seemed in good health, but he was tired and having nightmares, which seems not surprising. Delhi was becoming somewhat more normal, though murders were still a common occurrence. Few Muslims came to visit Gandhi or attended his prayer meetings. He began to feel useless in Delhi and talked of wandering through India, but the idea was nothing but a symptom of his restless search for ways to bring peace. The end of it, inevitable by now, was another fast.

Only by heightening drama could Gandhi gain the power he needed to bring about peace. First there were radio broadcasts about his reasons for fasting. The peace of India had been destroyed. No Muslim was safe. If Hindus and Muslims in Delhi would devote themselves to peace without pressure from police or army, then he would eat.

The doctors now took over. Radio bulletins announced at intervals how many ounces of water he had drunk, how much urine he had passed, what he weighed, what headaches, cramps, or nausea he suffered from. He received many visitors; and while his strength permitted, he walked into the garden to hold his daily prayer meeting at five o'clock. Daily thereafter he spoke to the nation over the radio from his bed,

his voice getting weaker and hoarser until it was hardly
audible.

Meanwhile though he was fasting, the business of government had to go on. Cabinet meetings came to Birla House
and sat around Gandhi's bed, discussing whether to pay to
Pakistan a large cash balance that was owing as a result of
the partition, seeing that the two countries were now fighting
each other in Kashmir. The world was always pressing its
attention on the sick man. Hindu fanatics came up the road
to stop outside the house, crying, "Death to Gandhi!" He
sighed and began to recite the name of God.

Patel and Nehru were not getting on together, yet neither
of them could be dispensed with. Nehru was the man who
commanded the loyalty of the Congress Party and who had
the vision to lead the India of the future. Patel, though dis-
liked by most of his colleagues, was the strong man of the
hour, indispensable to restoring order and to pushing negotiations with the princes, who still hesitated over the terms
of their adherence to free India. Without either man there
would have been no government; yet matters were going so
badly between them that Patel wrote a letter to Gandhi
demanding that he stop his fast to examine the problem of
whether or not he, Patel, should resign.

Many people in Delhi were working for communal peace
against time, for Gandhi's kidneys soon failed to do their job,
and he had entered the danger zone. Rajendra Prasad, the
Patna lawyer who had helped Gandhi in Champaran and was
now the President of Congress, called leaders of every faction
to his house, urging them to make a bold gesture of friendship that would convince Gandhi that they meant to keep
the peace. Processions of Hindu-Muslim unity were organized to parade the streets. Nehru told a vast crowd that they

must save Bapu by establishing peace in Delhi. Rajendra Prasad got the signatures of a hundred and thirty community leaders to a document agreeing that the Muslims should have their possessions restored, that they should be welcome in Delhi, and that they should be protected by the community, not the police. With this in hand he approached the Hindu Mahasabha, the Sikhs, and other dissident groups for their signatures.

He succeeded in the nick of time. Gandhi was already delirious for some part of the night, and his voice had died away until it was almost indistinguishable. But he could still receive the leaders, listen to their agreement, and hear their arguments. Perhaps it was a patched-up peace, but it was genuinely meant. After prayers and chanting, Gandhi accepted a ceremonial glass of orange juice. Fruit was distributed to the guests, about a hundred in number, who had crowded in to receive his blessing. The fast was over, and Delhi was at peace.

Hai Rama!

G ANDHI SOON RECOVERED his energies. Even as he lay at the
point of death, he had made a resolution, which seemed to
harden in the next days, that as soon as he was able, he would
lead a peace march on Pakistan in hope of reuniting the
severed parts of India. He did not imagine that he would
survive the journey or even seriously expect to accomplish
anything. Jinnah had said no word about his fast, though it
had been undertaken for the sake of the Muslims in India.
He had answered none of Gandhi's messages relayed to him
through Suhrawardy's connections and had made no gesture
to deplore the treatment of Hindus in Pakistan. Gandhi did
not look for a miracle, but he obeyed his inner voice without
counting the cost.

He was perhaps glad to embrace a form of action that
would remove him from the capital. One of his tasks in the
next few days was to draw up a proposal for dissolving the
whole organization of the Congress party. Let Congress
renounce the struggle for power, give up corrupt bargaining.

and proclaim itself the servant of God. It seems possible that Gandhi was considering the construction of a new party in India, built on the foundation of such Gandhi creations as the All-India Spinners Federation. If he had lived, he might have led a peaceful opposition to the very politicians who owed him their power. So far, such ideas were only part of the confusion of the times as reflected in his mind. By going to Pakistan, he could put off a decision, possibly forever.

After breaking his fast, he was well enough to be carried down the garden in a chair, up onto a terrace where stood a small pavilion from which it was his custom to conduct a daily prayer meeting for those who cared to assemble. On the second day that he appeared, about three hundred people were present. The ceremony opened with prayers and chants, after which Gandhi made a short address, which was as usual broadcast by the All-India Radio. Since this was so soon after the fast, cameras were focused on him.

He was actually speaking in the low, hoarse voice that betrayed his lack of strength when an explosion about twenty-five yards from where he was sitting blew out part of the garden wall. Everybody turned to look, and Manu-behn in terror threw herself at Gandhi's feet. There was no panic, however; Gandhi merely supposed that the military were "practicing" somewhere. With the minimum of fuss, the police arrested a young man who had been seen lighting a fuse. By this time there was a little more confusion as some part of the audience walked out. The police let the people go unchallenged while they searched their prisoner, who proved to have a hand grenade on his person and admitted that he had come to kill Gandhi.

The conspirator was a young Punjabi called Madanlal Pahwa, twenty years old and a displaced person. He had seen his father and aunt murdered before his eyes by Punjabi

Muslims and had escaped to Delhi, unbalanced by the sight of unimaginable horrors. The police, correctly deducing that he did not have the resolution or intelligence to carry out such a murder alone, suspected a conspiracy. Before midnight, he had given them the names of his fellow plotters.

Curiously enough, Madanlal Pahwa was the only one of the conspirators who had been driven to the edge of madness by his sufferings in the Punjab at Muslim hands. The real leaders of the group, Nathuram Godse and Narayan Apte, were respectively editor and manager of a right-wing Hindu newspaper in Poona, single-minded and serious men in their middle thirties. Behind them stood a sinister figure in Bombay, whose extraordinary history had brought him in contact with Gandhi in 1909. This man was the Indian terrorist Savarkar, who had run what might be called a school for assassins in London and had directed a couple of political murders. Convicted of the second of these, he was sentenced in 1910 to imprisonment for life. The sentence, however, was commuted in 1924, and since than Savakar had risen to become the leader of the Hindu Mahasabha. This right-wing Hindu organization had in the beginning been chiefly directed against Gandhi on account of his attempts to reform Hinduism and in particular his campaigns for the untouchables. With the rise of Hindu-Muslim communal strife, however, the Mahasabha organization had concentrated on recruiting, arming, and training Hindu bullies to take revenge on Muslims. Savarkar was no longer its president, but he had great influence, particularly over better-educated members like Godse and Apte.

Their actual decision to kill Gandhi had been taken on or around Independence Day on the grounds that the partition of India was Gandhi's fault. Thus ironically enough he was held responsible for the one thing he fought hardest to prevent. On Independence Day, as we have seen, Gandhi was in Calcutta, still planning to go back to Noakhali. There was no telling where he would be by the time the conspirators had outlined a general plan and looked about for weapons. Godse leaned toward the view that eight or ten persons should all attack Gandhi at once, so as to be certain of finishing him off. This involved him and Apte in recruiting help, which in turn meant throwing out hints and watching reactions. Before the final group was organized, a few dozen people had been acquainted with the general plan, though not all with the name of the victim. In spite of this, however, the gathering of weapons was a serious difficulty. It was not until January 10, 1948, that the conspirators were outfitted. On the thirteenth, Gandhi began his fast in Delhi; and one of the objectives he announced was that of inducing the Indian government to hand over the 550 million rupees they owed to Pakistan. This so infuriated Godse that he decided Gandhi must be killed on his first public appearance if he survived the fast. Accordingly, the conspirators transferred themselves to Delhi, where they found hospitality among the Hindu Mahasabha, to a couple more of whom they confided their plans.

Though there was a guard at the main gate of Birla House with a small police box built to accommodate it, the side door to the garden and terrace was easy of access. People came and went all the time, so that the conspirators had no difficulty in getting in to look the place over. They decided that Pahwa should blow up the wall to cause a panic, while the others concealed themselves behind a screen that ran along the back of the pavilion, separating it from the servants' quarters. Through ventilation holes in the screen they would throw grenades at Gandhi, indifferent to the fate of those standing by him.

Pahwa performed his part, but the other conspirators were taken aback because no panic followed. Nor had they reckoned with the fact that cameras were trained on the pavilion which might easily record the features of the assassins. They made their way out of the garden and, as soon as they had opportunity, fled to Bombay.

Since it was clear that Gandhi's life had been attempted, Patel now posted a guard around Birla House. As, however, nobody felt able to tell Gandhi that he should not hold his public prayer meetings, strangers continued to walk into the garden. Guards mixed themselves among them, and plainclothes police were stationed along Gandhi's path as he came out of his quarters; but a determined man found little difficulty in approaching him. Meanwhile, though news had come in from Bombay that the conspirators had gathered there before coming on to Delhi, and though Savarkar's record and probable connection with the affair was known, nothing effective was done to trace the conspirators there. Patel, who ought to have given the matter his full attention, was involved in countless other urgent problems, including his continuing quarrel with Nehru. Many of the police were closely connected with right-wing organizations and may have been afraid of what investigation would reveal.

The failure of its first attempt reduced the number of resolute members of the conspiracy to three — Godse, Apte and a restaurant proprietor called Karkare who had been with a Mahasabha relief expedition to Noakhali, was deeply embittered by what he had seen, and hated Gandhi for preaching forgiveness. By this time Godse had decided that one resolute person would suffice to do the deed. He offered himself as the sacrifice, while yet he seemed to rely on the others to keep his courage up. Between them they had managed to lay their hands on two revolvers for the previous attempt, but both needed repair and could not be relied on. After another week of wild hunts and secret meetings, any of which ought to have brought about their arrest, they managed to buy a revolver in excellent condition. By this time they were once more in Delhi and ready to make another attempt. On January 30, Godse drove up to Birla House at about 4:30 in a hired carriage, dressed in a green pullover and khaki jacket. A few minutes later Apte and Karkare, who had agreed to give moral support to Godse's attempt, drove up also and went into the garden to mix with the crowd.

Gandhi woke at his usual early hour for prayer and meditation before working through the early part of the morning on a draft constitution for Congress, which he handed to his secretary before breakfast. He was planning in the next day or so to go back to Sevagram, where he hoped to recover his strength. He knew, however, that his presence was still needed in Delhi to help preserve the peace; and he proposed to return in about two weeks' time. Most of his day was spent in conferences, or in receiving visitors, who included an American photographer. At four o'clock he received Patel, with whom he spoke about making peace with Nehru. After the prayer meeting he was going to see Nehru and discuss the whole quarrel with him. He wanted the two to reach an agreement that very day. This was an absorbing conversation and of the utmost importance, causing even Gandhi, who lived by his watch, to forget the time. It was ten minutes past five when Patel left, and Gandhi was annoyed with his nieces for not interrupting him. He should have been dead by now, according to his own timing.

Since he could not yet walk without support, he came down the long path from the house to the side of the terrace with his arms around the shoulders of his nieces. It took him about three minutes, although he was hurrying to make up for lost time. He was teasing Abhabehn about her cooking, pretending that she was serving him cattle fare and remarking, "Is it not grand of me to relish what no one else cares for?"

So saying, he came to six brick steps, which led up to the grassy terrace on which a few hundred people waited for the prayers. They had crowded forward to watch him; but as he got to the top, they fell back a little in order to let him pass through to the pavilion. Gandhi took his arms from his nieces' shoulders and folded his hands with palms together, in the traditional Hindu greeting, saying nothing, as he smiled at the crowd.

As he did so, a man in a khaki coat pushed forward so roughly that he knocked out of Manubehn's hand Gandhi's spectacle case, his wooden prayer beads, notebook and spit-

Gandhi, still weak from his fast, shares a joking moment with his nieces

toon, which she was carrying. People used to run forward to Gandhi in a crouching position before they fell to kiss his feet, so that Manubehn was only slightly disturbed by his roughness. "Brother," she remonstrated, "Bapuji is already late for prayers. Why are you bothering him?"

She had hardly uttered the words before Godse, still crouched over his pistol but now looking upward at Gandhi, fired three shots pointblank, the first into his abdomen and the other two into his chest. Bloodstains appeared on his white shawl as he cried with a last effort, "Hai Rama! Hai Rama!" ("Oh God! Oh God!") and collapsed onto the grass, his hands still folded. The distracted girls knelt down to gather his head onto their laps, but he made no movement. Blood still poured from his wounds, and his skin turned from brown to gray. About ten minutes later, men carried him back to Birla House and laid him on the floor, where the two girls once more cradled his head as they waited for a doctor.

No Ordinary Light

The news of Gandhi's murder traveled fast. Patel, summoned back to the house he had just left, found it necessary to convince the distraught girls that Bapu was dead beyond all hope of revival. When Nehru appeared, he was so overcome that he actually clung to Patel for comfort. Meanwhile, thousands had begun to crowd into the gardens of Birla House. Faces pressed at the windows of the little annex until those inside feared the glass would break. Over the hymns that were being chanted around the body, the movements of the crowd outside could be heard. There was much sobbing, and occasionally a thundering shout of "Victory to Mahatma Gandhi" would be raised.

Devadas was the only one of the sons in Delhi. Ramdas was in Nagpur; Manilal in South Africa. No one knew the whereabouts of Harilal. It was in the presence of Devadas, therefore, that funeral arrangements were discussed. Lord Mountbatten, Nehru and other members of Congress were in favor of embalming the body and permitting it to lie in state in different parts of the country to content the millions of people who might wish a final sight of their Mahatma. But Pyarelal, Gandhi's secretary, who had been closest to him, maintained that he had given strict instructions that his body be not embalmed, but cremated in the usual Hindu way as soon as he died. So emphatic was Pyarelal about Gandhi's express wishes that no one could contradict him. In the Indian climate, cremation customarily follows within twenty-four hours of death, so that funeral arrangements were put in hand for the following morning.

Outside, the ever-growing crowd was becoming insistent that they see Gandhi for the last time. He was accordingly carried up to the roof, where he was displayed with an army searchlight trained upon him. Covered from the waist down with a white cloth, but naked above it, he looked very much as men had always seen him, except that his face had fallen in with loss of blood, making him look smaller than ever.

They carried him down again some hours later to prepare his corpse for the burning. They painted a mark on his forehead and put his wooden beads and a garland of yarn about his neck. Gandhi had always refused presents and had even revolted against the Indian custom of welcoming people with a garland of flowers. In his practical way he had let it be known that the only garland that could please him would be one of homespun yarn. Now he lay with yarn about his neck as men anointed him with sandalwood paste and wrote "Hai Rama" in rose petals near his head and the sacred word *Om* at his feet. They placed him on the roof again for the crowds to gaze upon, while the sun rose through heavy clouds on his last day.

No organization except the military was capable of staging a funeral parade of over a million. Thus, by the irony of fate, he who had wanted to supersede armies was drawn to his pyre in a military truck, a huge American army weapons carrier towed by selected men from the armed forces of his country and accompanied by soldiers, airmen, policemen, sailors, and the mounted bodyguard of the Governor General. Overhead flew military planes scattering roses.

Behind the military came an enormous procession, trailing out a couple of miles behind the coffin. Every organization in Delhi was represented, as well as many others from all around the country. The start had been delayed until eleven to wait for the arrival of Ramdas, and in the interval crowds poured into the town on foot, by bullock cart, by train or plane. They had started as soon as Nehru, struggling hoarsely with his tears, had broken the news over the All-India Radio. "The light has gone out of our lives," he told the people, "and there is darkness everywhere."

Gandhi had complained in life that a five-minute journey from train to automobile could take an hour. It took five hours to bring him to his funeral pyre through the wide streets of New Delhi, built for processions, but never for such a procession as this. A million people were out in the streets to watch, jamming the windows of the buildings, climbing the telegraph poles, draping themselves over statuary, bending the branches of the trees that shaded Delhi's avenues. The packed crowds pushing forward showed small respect for the armed police and armored cars that had been stationed everywhere, not only to preserve the dignity of the dead man, but to guard against further attempts on Nehru and the other leaders of the nation, who were standing on the weapons carrier on guard around the bier. Time and again the tide of human beings overflowed the route and brought the car to a standstill until Nehru, disdaining precautions for his personal safety, jumped down into the road and ordered the people to show their respect for Bapu by moving back.

At four o'clock that afternoon the head of the endless procession reached the cremation spot, a small brick platform erected on the bank of the Jumna River and surrounded at a distance of a hundred yards by a stout barricade. Behind this people had been jammed since early that morning, many fainting or being injured in the crush. From time to time a section of the barrier would give way, and guards of the Royal Indian Air Force would assemble inside to push the people back.

The preliminaries did not take long. People lifted the body onto the platform, arranging the scented logs of sandalwood around it, sprinkling it with holy water, incense, leaves, and flowers while a priest recited sacred verses. Then Ramdas lit the pyre with flaming camphor. It flared high as the crowd began to shout, "Mahatmaji has become immortal!"

When nothing was left but glowing coals, barbed wire was erected to keep the people away, and a guard was set. Some of the crowd remained all night, and unrecognized among them appeared the wasted shape of Harilal Gandhi, dying slowly of tuberculosis. The ashes of his father went on glowing after he left.

Not for thirteen days was the pyre disturbed. The ashes were then gathered up and parts distributed to all the separate provinces of India. Such bones as were not consumed were placed in a copper urn and carried by special train to Allahabad, where the Ganges, the Jumna, and the invisible celestial river meet. There they were cast into the water, making Gandhi, as far as could be arranged, a part of all-India.

This was not all the history of Gandhi, however. As Nehru said of him: "The light has gone out, I said, and yet I was wrong. For the light that shone in this country was no ordinary light. The light that has illumined this country for many years will illumine this country for many more years, and a thousand years later that light will still be seen in this country, and the world will see it and it will give solace to innumerable hearts. For that light represented the living truth, and the eternal man was with us with his eternal truth, reminding us of the right path, drawing us from error, taking this ancient country to freedom."

What, then, became of the light? The military funeral, loaded with the panoply of a great modern state, symbolized an India different from Gandhi's dream. This was the India that was bound to have become free in the forties, for it is not conceivable that the British Empire of the East could have survived the Second World War, especially after the conquests of the Japanese. Had Gandhi never lived, this India must have arisen. Yet when it did arise, his mark was on it everywhere.

First of all, the light illumined the leaders. No one but Gandhi could have chosen, used, and kept on one team men so incompatible as Nehru, the sensitive, liberalized politician, and Patel, the rough, right-wing political boss. Yet it fell to Patel after Gandhi's death to make a nation out of the hodgepodge of British provinces and outmoded princely states. To Nehru fell the task of leading and directing the India thus created. It was a time when both men were needed, yet it was only Gandhi who kept them together. What was more, the unity imposed on the two leaders extended throughout Congress. Gandhi had found Congress a place of faction; he left it as a party, with diverse points of view, yet one common interest. Congress had and has many faults. It was not the association of the Servants of God that Gandhi desired, and his disappointment in Congress clouded his last days. Notwithstanding, he had made the Congress party the only instrument capable of governing united India.

In another sense, too, his light fell on the leaders of the nation. Despite the corruption that came with the achievement of power and the era of jobs for the boys, there were people who rose above these things, inspired by Gandhi. In 1917, Rajendra Prasad had been a hardheaded, practical lawyer in Patna whose servants would not permit Gandhi to use his latrine or well. Realistically he had complained that the middle classes were not remarkable for acts of public service. Yet he had worked in Champaran with Gandhi and had changed his life. Rajendra Prasad became the first president of free India and set an example by living simply in a little corner of his vast official mansion, rising in the spirit of Gandhi above power and pomp.

Such influences were vital to the nation. It is true that India since independence has developed into a modern state that is facing away from the primitive, rural society that Gandhi envisaged. Hand-spinning and weaving have become craft work, no longer attempting to clothe the multitudes or free the peasant from the crushing burden of his poverty. Yet concern with agriculture, village sanitation, and education does persist. Gandhi created a government conscious that the dwellers in the towns are not all of India. The masses are rural. Similarly, though caste restrictions continue and prejudice dies hard, the government has been generous with special scholarships for the untouchables. It is aware of this problem also because of Gandhi.

Sevagram, "Service Village," did not long endure. It was natural that the community should break up with the loss of the strong will that held it together. But the activities of village life in Sevagram, the new latrines, the Gandhian school, the spinning and weaving did not persist either. Old ways were easier, and a government school a few miles off prepared the young for better jobs. Individuals who had lived with Gandhi at Sevagram and elsewhere did devote themselves to lives of service, but often with only moderate good fortune. Mirabehn, for instance, gave the next ten years of her life to working for better treatment of Indian cows, thereby attempting reform of religious custom and an important service to Indian agriculture. But the government cared for this work, too; and government support meant regulations that Mirabehn found contrary to Gandhi's spirit. She gave up at last, left India, and rediscovered her old affinity for Beethoven.

It was not on Mirabehn, but on Vinoba Bhave that the mantle of Gandhi fell. In 1951, he was inspired to call a meeting in a village that had been disturbed by peasant rioting and ask whether some of the wealthy would not donate land to support their poorer brethren. A man stepped forward to offer a hundred acres. Next morning, Bhave went on to another village and was promised twenty-five more. He has been moving ever since. Somewhere in India a lean and aging man, accompanied by a couple of secretaries, a few disciples, and a drummer will appear on foot to hold a meeting and ask the villagers for land. Bhave calculated that his "Land-Gift" movement needed fifty million acres to support all landless peasants, supposing that their numbers did not grow substantially. In nineteen years or so, he has received about six million acres, some half of which have been useless for cultivation. But three million acres of good land have been given, which Bhave has formed into collective farms, connecting them with farmers' cooperatives. In the seven hundred thousand villages of India, three million acres may not make much difference. Yet as the free gift of land-hungry peasants to poor neighbors,

Vinoba Bhave's acres mean a great deal. The spirit of Gandhi, which is in a way the spirit of India, is far from dead.

The great failure of Gandhi's life was the partition of India and the creation of a breach which is not likely to be filled. Yet there are many Muslims still in the Indian Republic, and the government is as careful as the British used to be about offending their customs. Some say they are too careful and that just as Hinduism long remained backward because the British could do nothing to reform it, so the Muslims in India today are a backward class. But Gandhi would not care much about this sort of social problem as long as the Hindus were at pains to treat all Muslims as their brothers.

The light that Nehru spoke of shines in India in countless ways where Gandhi is remembered. But it shines on the twentieth century, too, and is reflected in those very westernized and industrial nations from which he turned away. In these, the spirit of nonviolent resistance has taken root, even though in many cases, Gandhi might not have recognized his child. What he developed was not the perfect answer to war or tyranny. It was already obvious during the Second World War that Gandhi had no universal solution to these bitter evils. We cannot forget his own sad words in Calcutta, "I cannot tell them that violence is wrong, while I cannot give them a substitute." What Gandhi had developed was a political method of protest particularly suited to minority or powerless groups under the government of a westernized democracy where protest is permitted. The techniques of Gandhi have been used by Indians against the government of free India. They have been used in the United States to express discrimination. They have attracted much of the vitality of Christian churches in various countries.

With the development of nonviolent protest by other

hands than Gandhi's, its nature has often changed. Gandhi, himself a born fighter, was never quite definite about what violence was — whether, for instance, he might approve the seizure of a building, the cutting of telegraph wires, or the destruction of machinery. On the commencement of the Second World War by Hitler's invasion of Poland, he even described the hopeless armed resistance of gallant Poles as "almost nonviolent." He was never quite certain what personal emergency might justify self-defense, and spent much time discussing imaginary crises with his disciples. Naturally it follows that if Gandhi himself found it difficult to draw a hard line between fighting with violence and without it, lesser men will be confused.

Another difficulty that has developed in the use of Gandhi's twentieth-century weapon is the confusion of its aims and objects. To Gandhi the object of a political protest was primarily a political one. Yet even Gandhi used a fast to campaign for social justice toward untouchables, and on a personal level he disciplined the boys of Sabarmati by fasting against them. Gandhi admitted that the nonviolent protester would have to decide about what was worth protesting, but he did not ever meet the argument that if everyone thinks he is right, the result will be confusion. In Gandhi's own lifetime the force of his personality was such that his will was seldom crossed. He could spend as much time as he wished on deciding what was the right thing to do, in perfect confidence that India would follow his direction. Furthermore, he was one of those men to whom truth appears simple, so that he was often less than understanding of a good man who did not agree with him. He could not admit that there might be genuine confusion between protesters, each in his own way right.

Jesus, perceiving his mission more clearly than Gandhi,

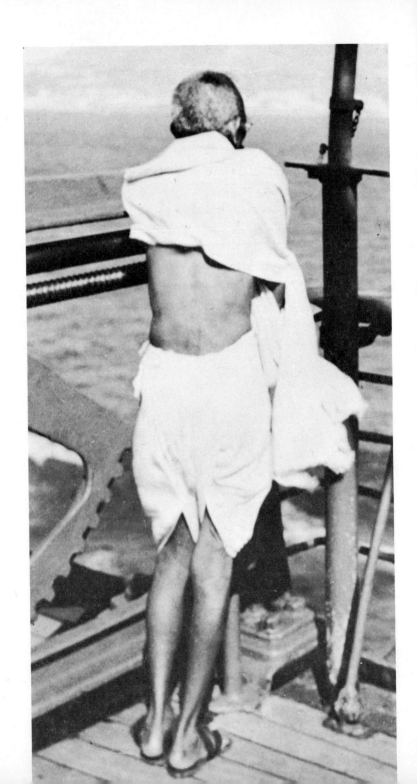

announced, "I came not to bring peace, but a sword."
Gandhi, too, though a man of peace, was a revolutionary. He
was less a composer of quarrels than a man who knew how
to give grievance its expression. Gandhi has presented the
world not with solutions, but with human attitudes of com-
passion, anger, self-sacrifice, and determination to right
wrong. He has given vitality to twentieth-century life, power
to the individual. Sometimes he has done this at the expense
of something else we value, namely law and order. He has
shaken us, however, out of too-rigid attitudes, questioned our
acceptance of things because they are so. By his life he has
warned us that the indulgence of nonviolent protest must be
paid for in self-discipline. Nor can he be blamed if men do
not learn this part of his lesson, for none could have applied
it more ruthlessly, both to himself and to other people.

We are grateful to United Press International
for permission to include photographs found on
pages 31, 114, 126, 141, 163, 173, 202, 237,
243, and 253; and to Wide World Photos for the
use of photographs found on pages ii, 9, 21,
79, 106, 159, 180, 184, 188, 209, 213, 222, and 264.

GLOSSARY OF INDIAN TERMS

Ba	Mother.
Bapu	Father.
Dhoti	Cloth worn by Indians below the waist, either forming a long skirt or divided into loose trousers or loincloth.
Goondas	Hooligans.
Harijans	"Children of God," a phrase coined by Gandhi for the outcastes.
Hartal	Day of mourning when all abstain from work. A one-day strike.
Khadi	Home-woven cloth made out of homespun yarn. The uniform of Gandhi's supporters.
Khilafat	The Caliphate or office of the Caliph, the spiritual head of the Muslim world.
Lathi	Indian police truncheon, a wooden staff tipped with metal.
Mahatma	Great Soul, a complimentary title given to Gandhi by Rabindranath Tagore.
Maulana	Complimentary title given to learned Muslims.
Pandit	Scholar, a complimentary title given to Nehru.
Ram or Rama	God.
Satyagraha	Truth Force, Gandhi's name for nonviolent non-cooperation.
Satyagrahi	One who practices *Satyagraha*.

Swaraj	Home Rule. *Hind Swaraj,* the title of Gandhi's book, means "Indian Home Rule."
Suffixes	-bai and -ba are common suffixes for a woman's name. -bai is applied to younger women (Kastur-bai) and -ba to older women (Putliba). For the sake of clarity Kasturbai is called Kastur*bai* throughout the book.

-behn means "aunt" and is generally applied as a token of respect, rather like Miss or Mrs. Mira-behn, Manubehn, and Abhabehn are examples.

-ji is a suffix showing respect or affection. Gandhi was usually called "Mahatma Gandhi" or "Gand-hiji" by the crowd.

INDEX